BOOK • VIDEO

HOT LICKS

EMILY REMLER

BEBOP AND SWING GUITAR

To access video visit:
www.halleonard.com/mylibrary

Enter Code
8132-7952-0962-6085

ISBN: 978-1-5400-6968-9

Visit Hal Leonard Online at
www.halleonard.com

Contact us:
Hal Leonard
7777 West Bluemound Road
Milwaukee, WI 53213
Email: info@halleonard.com

In Europe, contact:
Hal Leonard Europe Limited
42 Wigmore Street
Marylebone, London, W1U 2RN
Email: info@halleonardeurope.com

In Australia, contact:
Hal Leonard Australia Pty. Ltd.
4 Lentara Court
Cheltenham, Victoria, 3192 Australia
Email: info@halleonard.com.au

CONTENTS

BIOGRAPHY

In his book *Waiting for Dizzy*, Canadian music critic Gene Lees accurately described Emily Remler as a "superb musician and on her way to being a great one." Indeed, at the time of her sudden death at age 32, she had already begun developing her own distinct style of jazz guitar.

Born in Englewood Cliffs, New Jersey, in 1957, Remler grew up listening to folk and rock music. But while attending Berklee College of Music in the 1970s, she discovered the jazz recordings of Charlie Christian, Paul Desmond, and most notably, Wes Montgomery, whose work would prove to be a major influence on the blossoming young guitarist.

After graduation, Remler undertook a second musical education. She moved to New Orleans, where she quickly immersed herself in the city's historically eclectic blues and jazz scene. It was there that she met jazz guitar great Herb Ellis, who brought her to the 1978 Concord Jazz Festival, where she shared the stage with Ellis and jazz guitar legends Tal Farlow, Charlie Byrd, and Barney Kessel.

In 1979, Remler returned to New York, where she worked with singers Nancy Wilson and Astrud Gilberto. In the early 1980s, she signed with Concord Records and toured with David Benoit, also leading several of her own ensembles. Along the way, she was recognized as *Down Beat's* Guitarist of the Year, in 1985. She released five albums with Concord, but switched to Justice for the release of her final album, *This Is Me*, in 1990.

Remler, who had battled a longtime heroin addiction, died of a heart attack in Sydney, Australia, on May 4, 1990.

SELECT DISCOGRAPHY

Firefly (Concord Jazz, 1981)

Take Two (Concord Jazz, 1982)

Transitions (Concord Jazz, 1983)

Catwalk (Concord Jazz, 1984)

East to Wes (Concord Jazz, 1988)

This Is Me (Justice, 1990)

SUGGESTED LISTENING

Emily Remler *Firefly* (Concord, 1981); *This Is Me* (Justice, 1990)

Larry Coryell with Emily Remler *Together* (Concord, 1985)

Wes Montgomery *Smoking at the Half Note* (Verve, 1965);
Boss Guitar (Riverside, 1963)

Pat Martino *Essence* (Muse, 1973); *Starbright* (Warner Bros., 1976)

Joe Pass *Virtuoso* (Pablo, 1973)

Chapter 1: Rhythm

Example 1
(1:02)

Example 2
(2:57)

Example 3
(3:56)

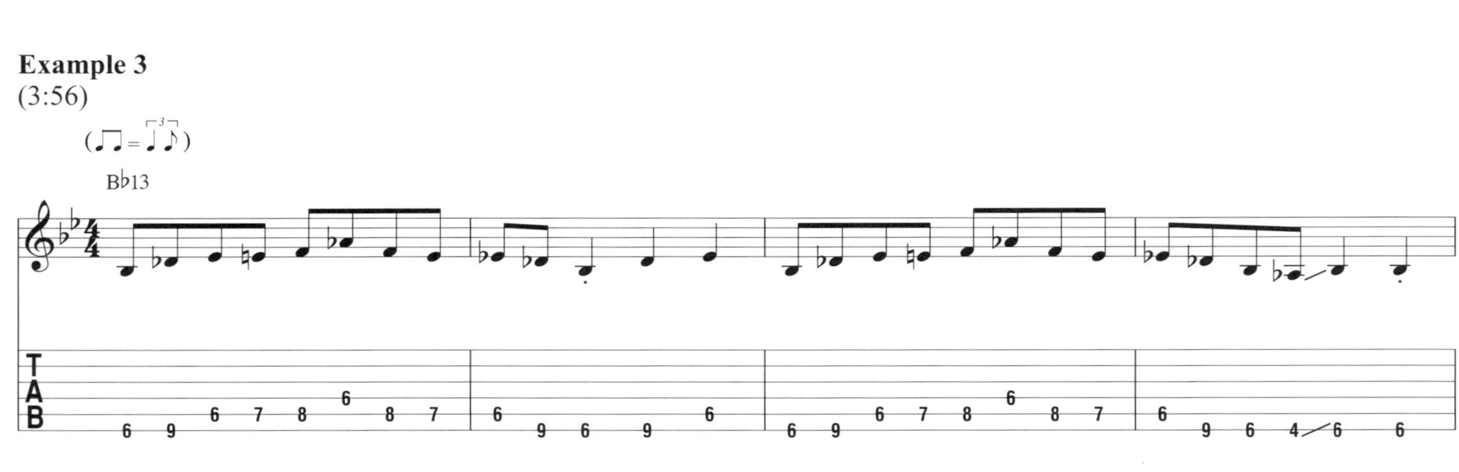

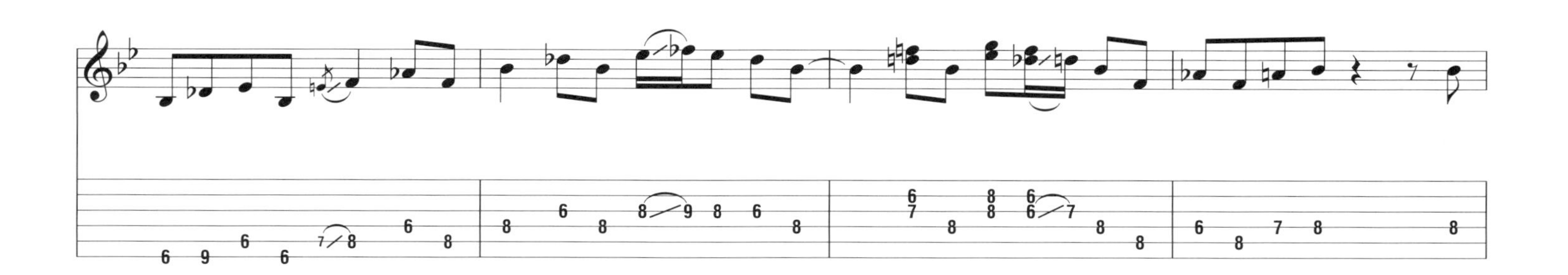

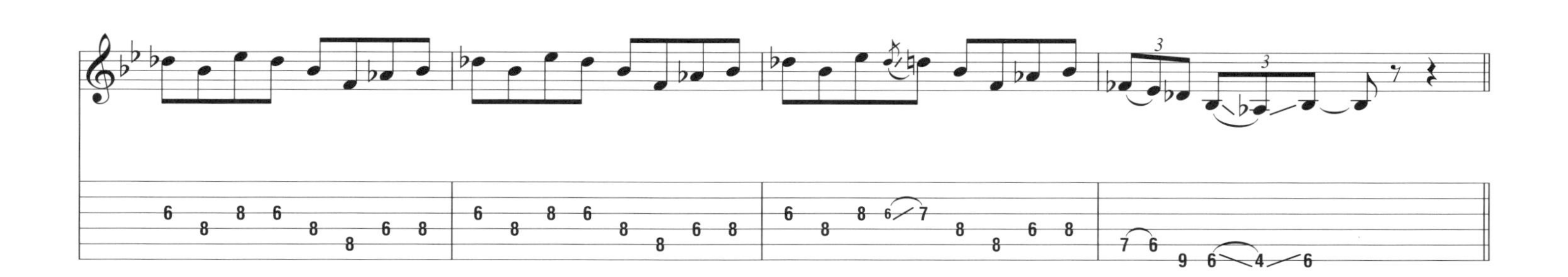

Example 4
(5:19)

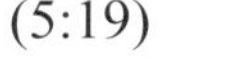

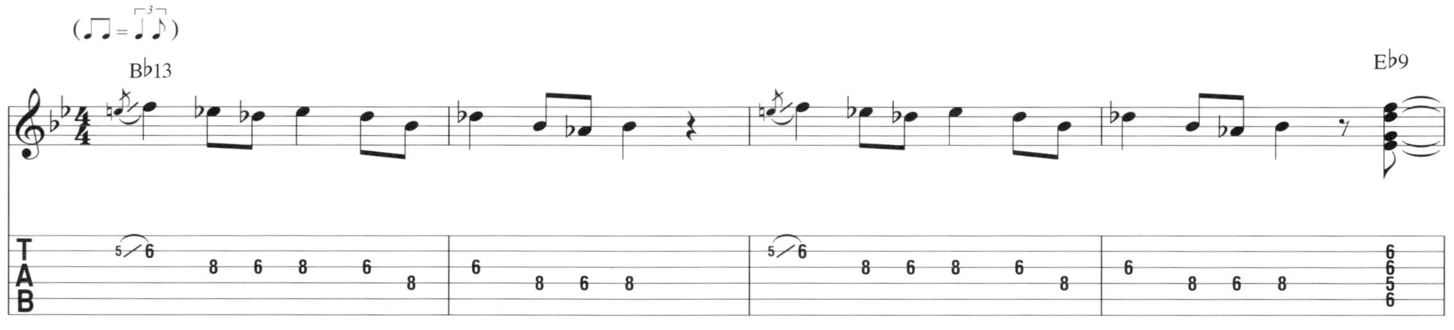

Example 5
(5:57)

Example 6
(8:58)

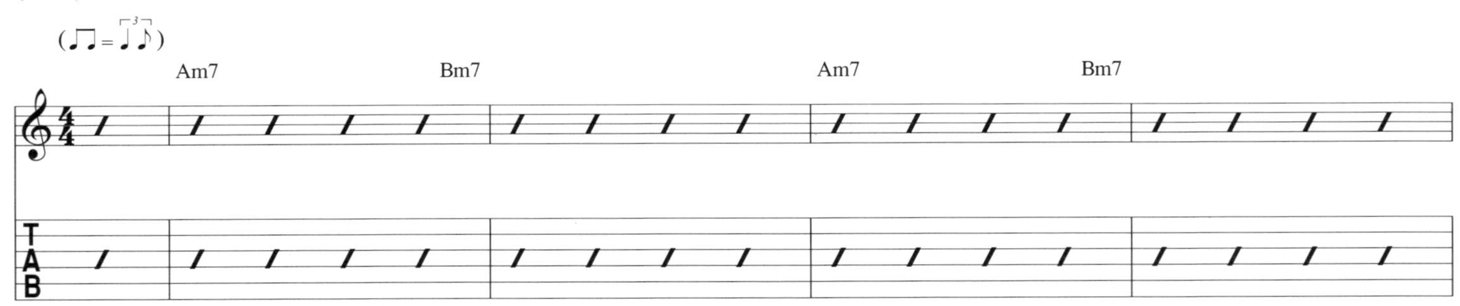

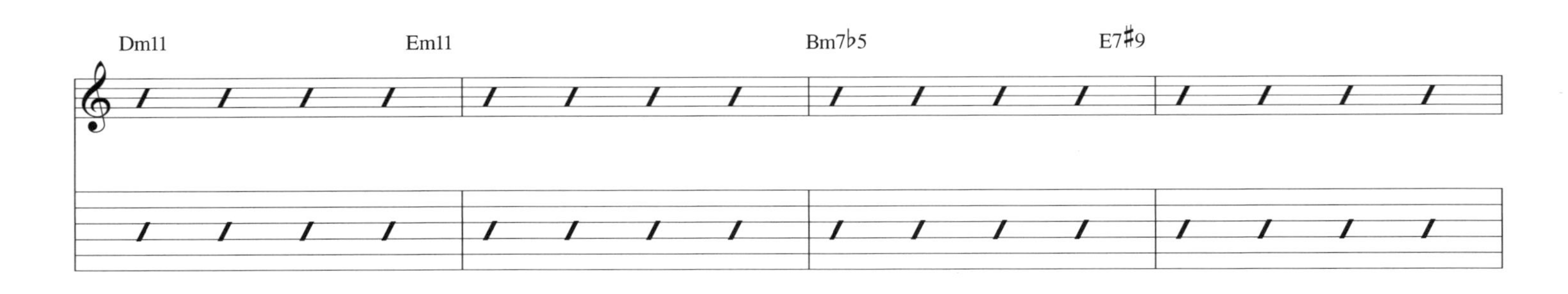

Am7
Bm7
Am7
D9
Am7
D9
E9
Am7
E7♯9
Am7
Bm7
Am7
Bm7
Dm11
Em11
Bm11
E7♯9/B
Am7
Bm7
Am7
D9
Am7
D9
E9
Am7
E7♯9

Chapter 2: Guide Tones, Part 1

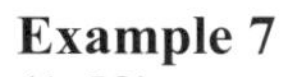

Example 7
(1:52)

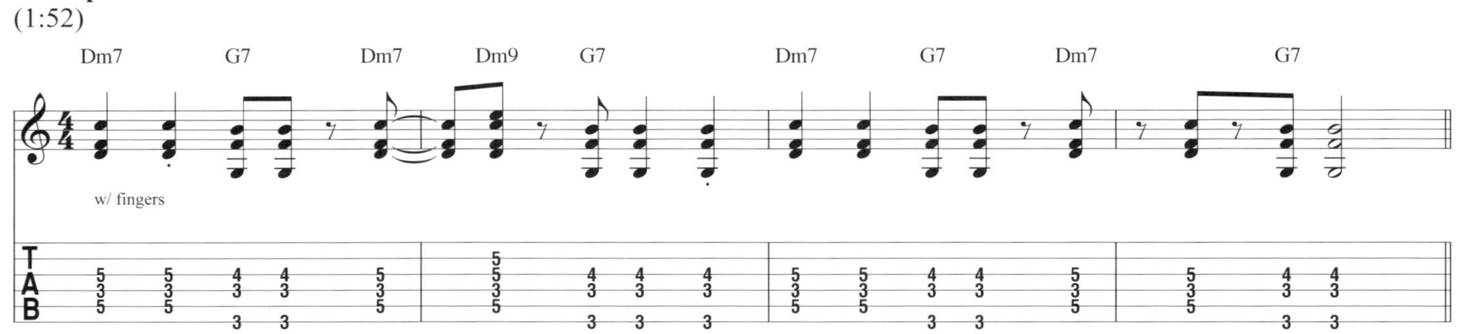

Example 8
(2:04)

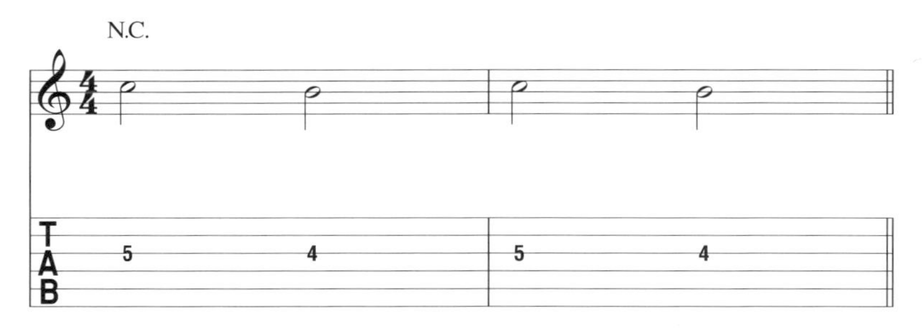

Example 9
(2:44)

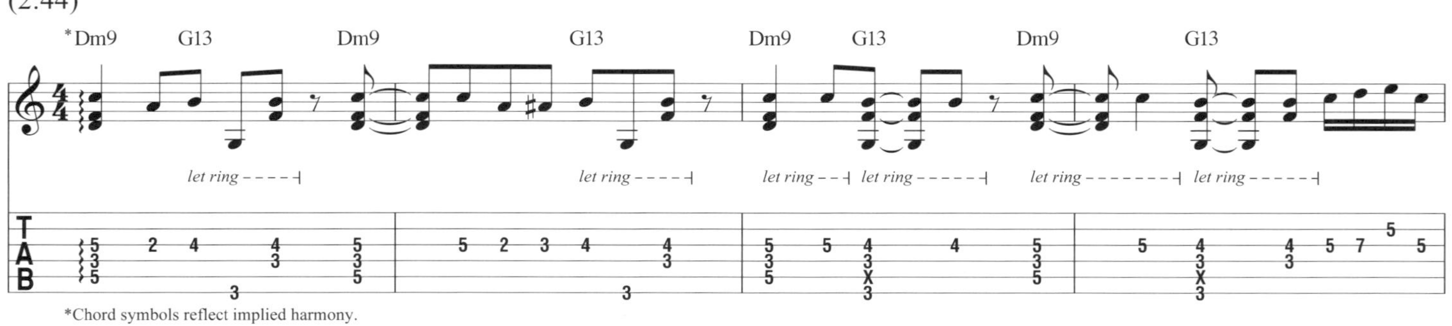

*Chord symbols reflect implied harmony.

Dm9 G13 Dm9 G13 Dm9 G13 Dm9 G13

Example 10
(3:11)

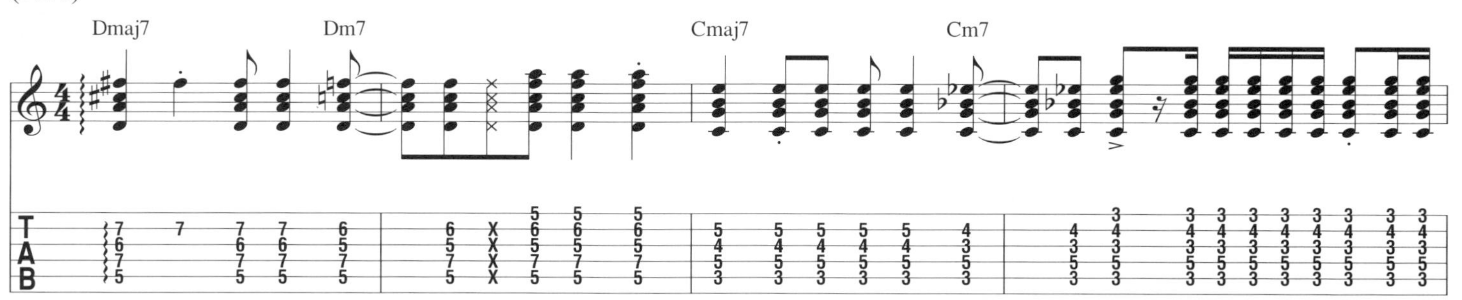

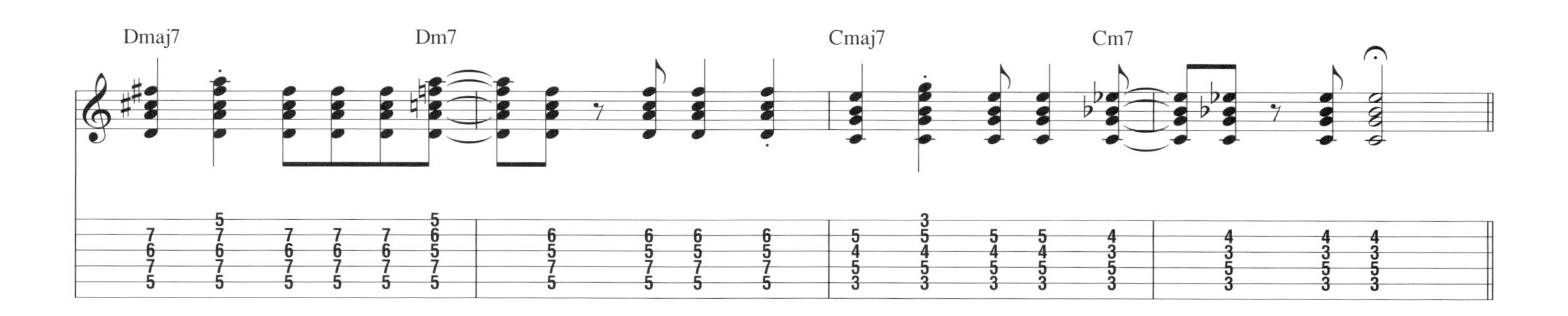

Example 11
(3:33)

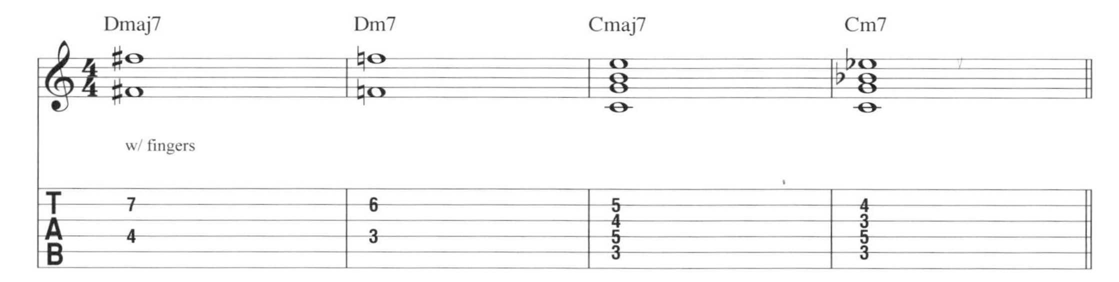

Example 12
(3:58)

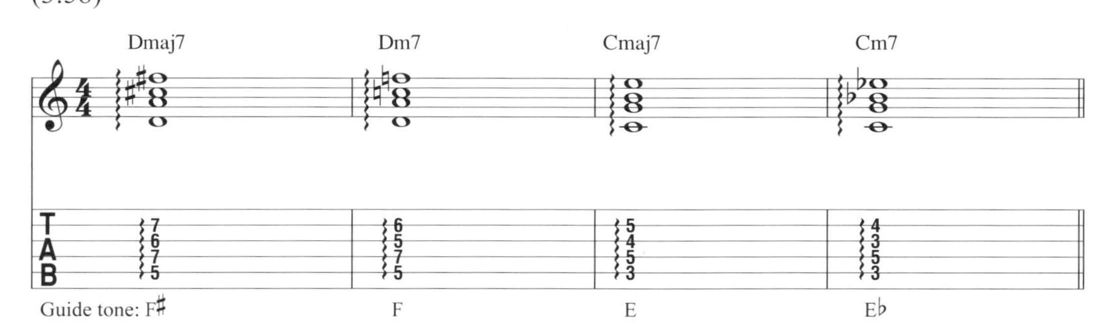

Example 13

(4:41)

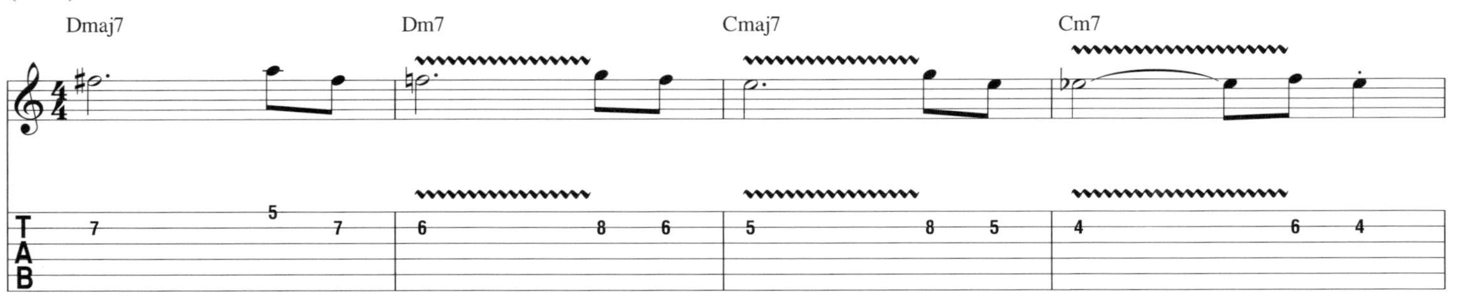

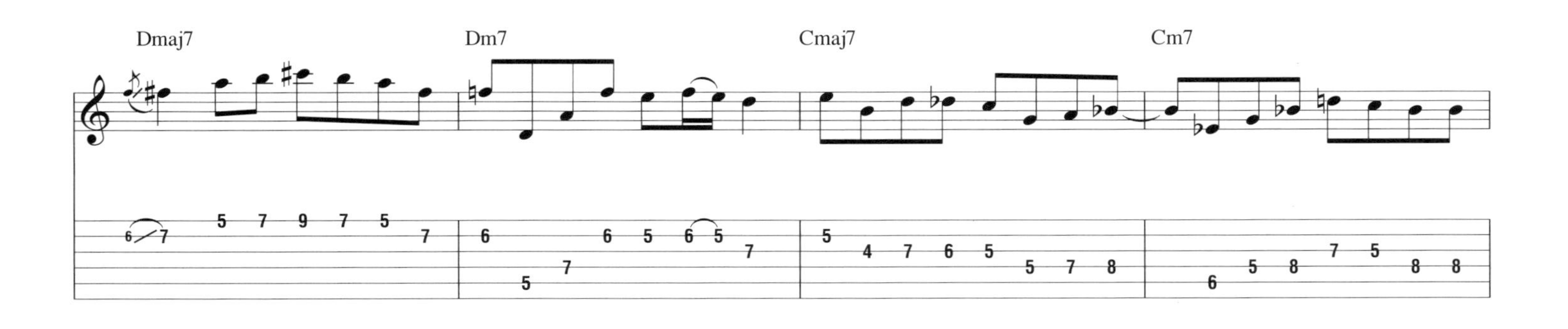

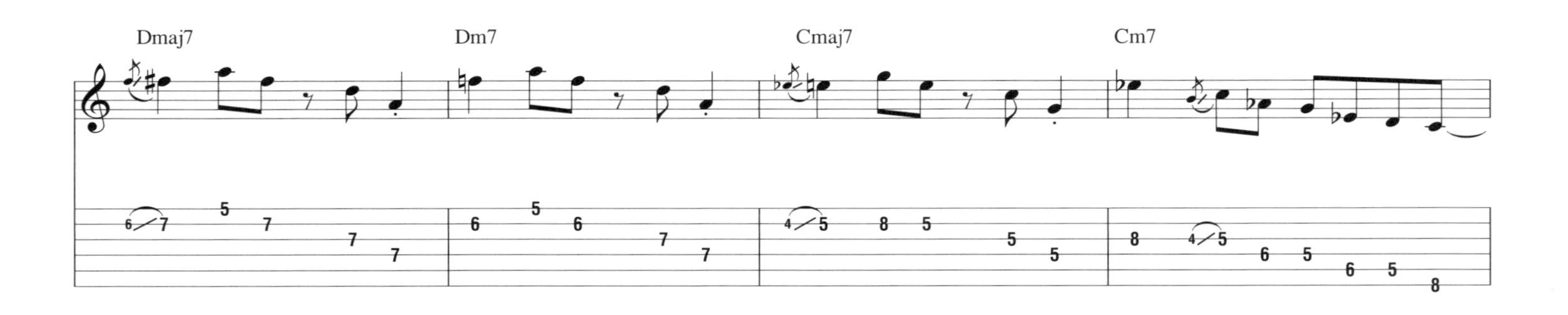

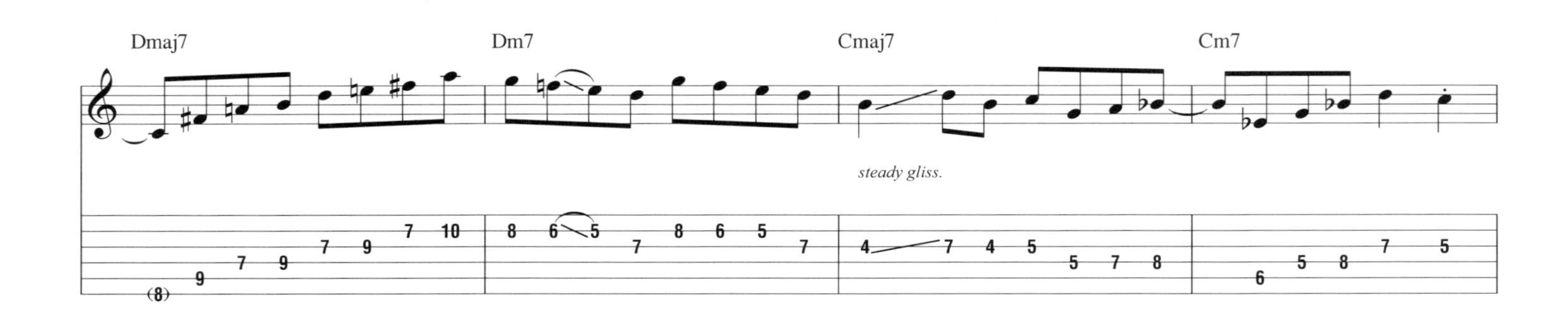

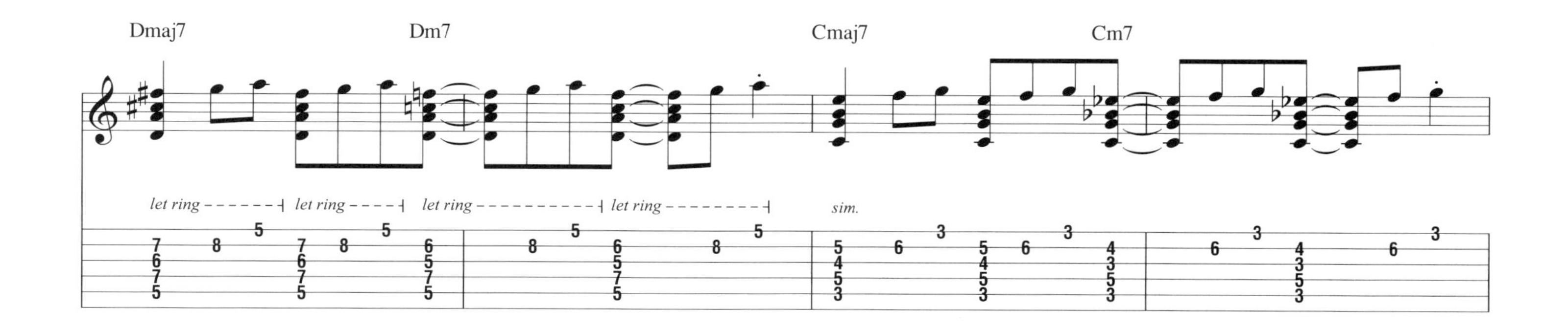

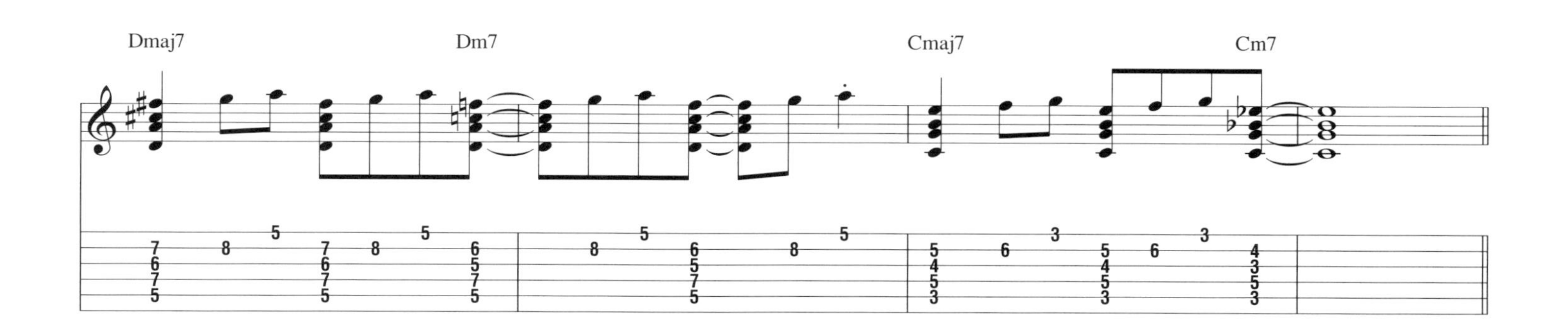

Example 14
(6:36)

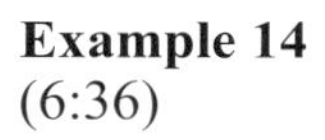

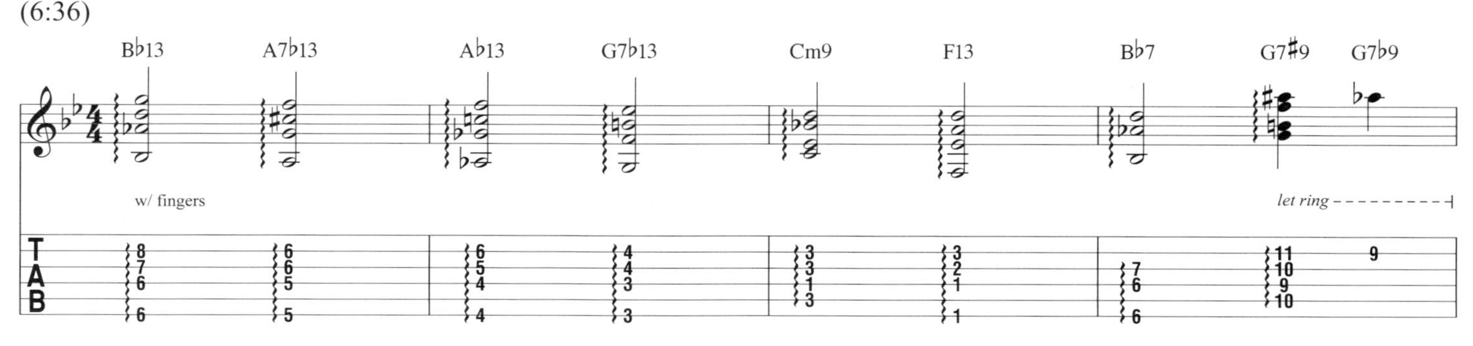

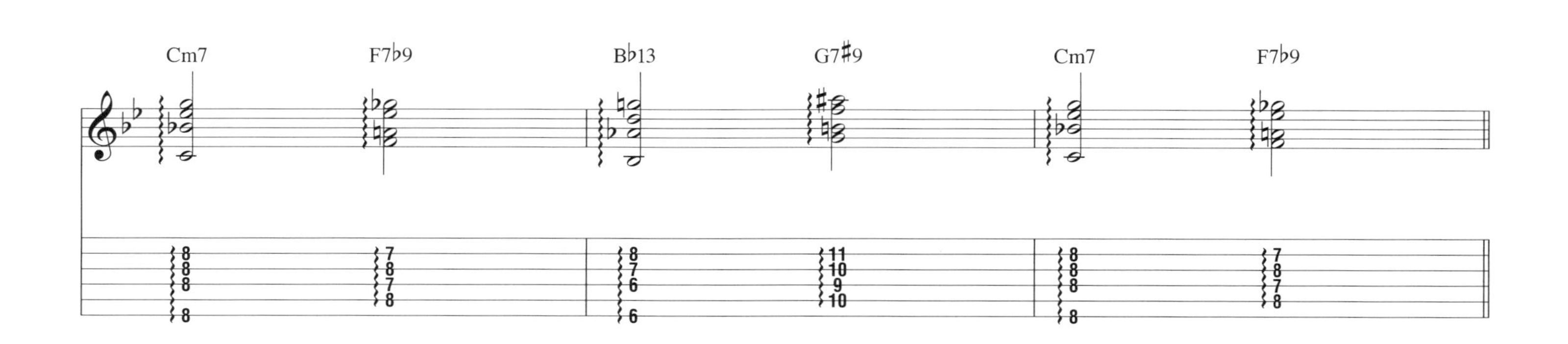

Chapter 3: Guide Tones, Part 2

Example 15
(1:03)

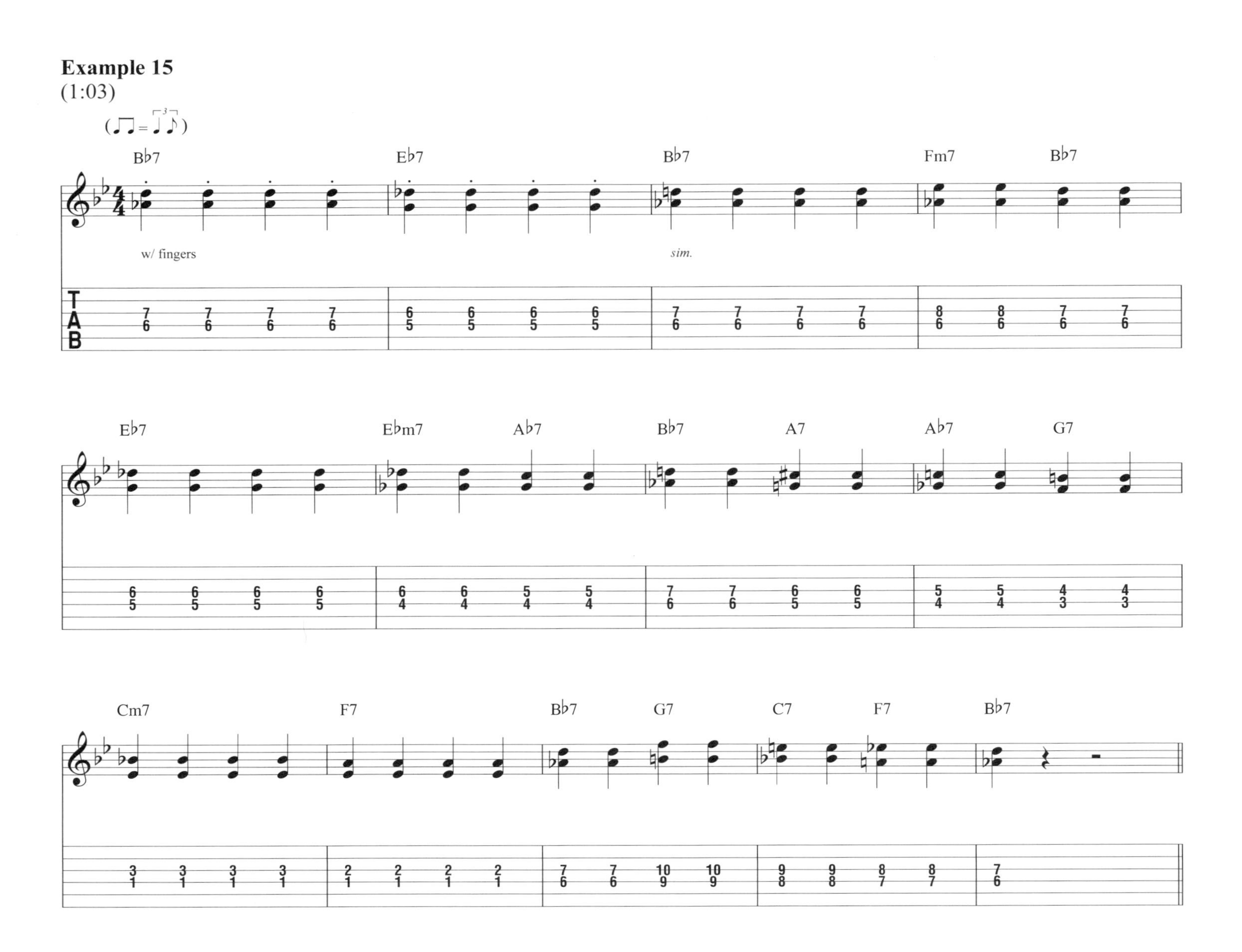

Example 16
(2:19)

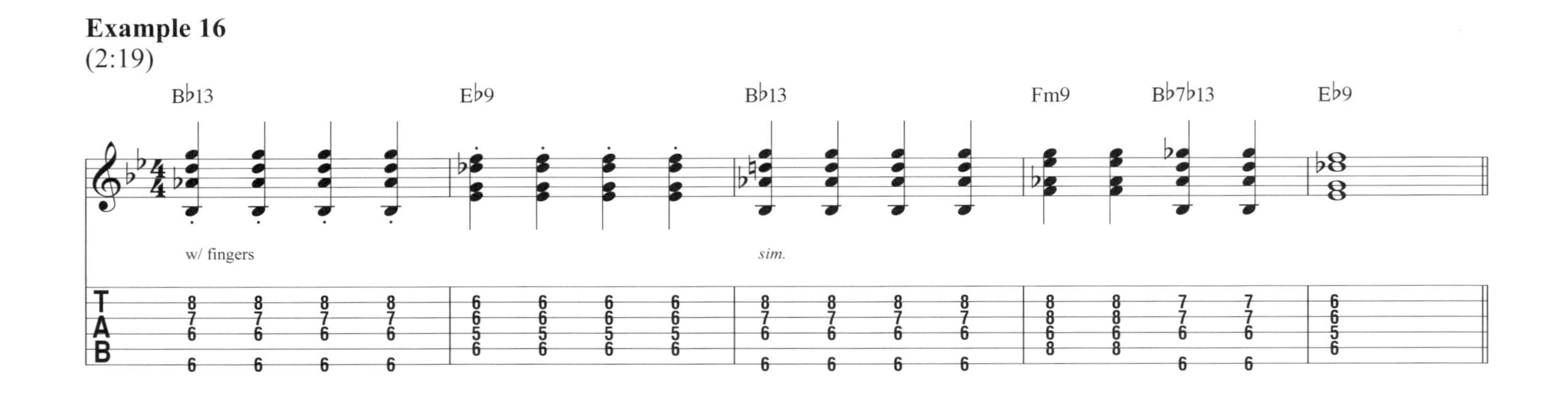

Example 17

(3:36)

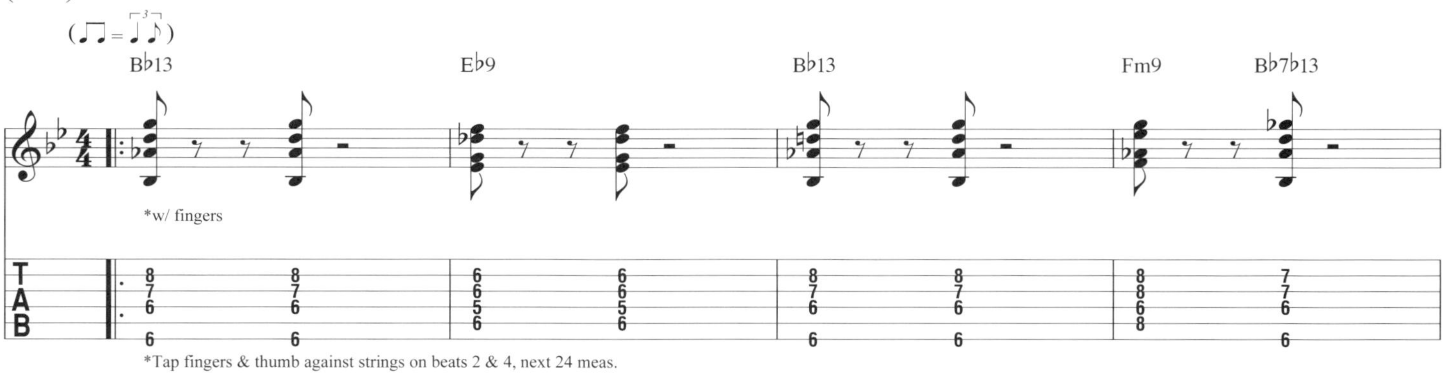

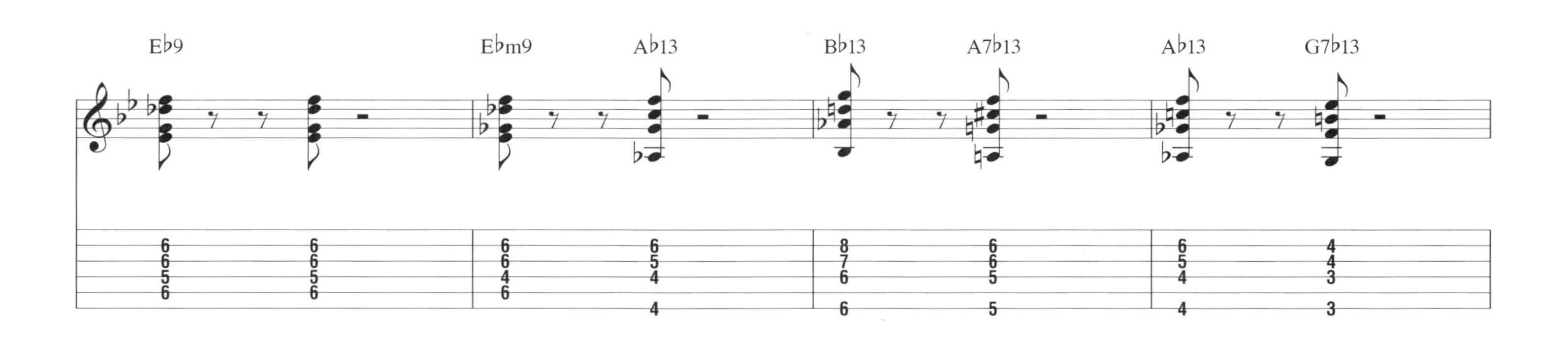

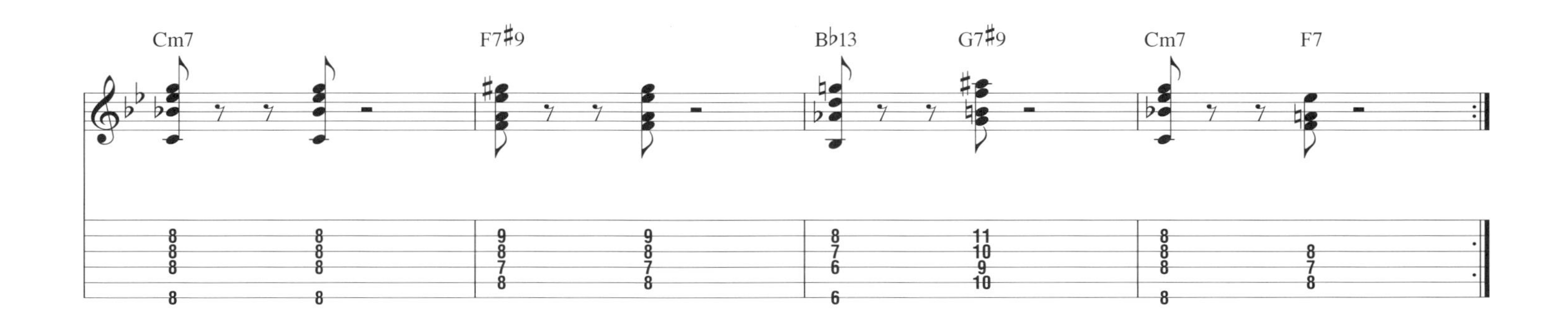

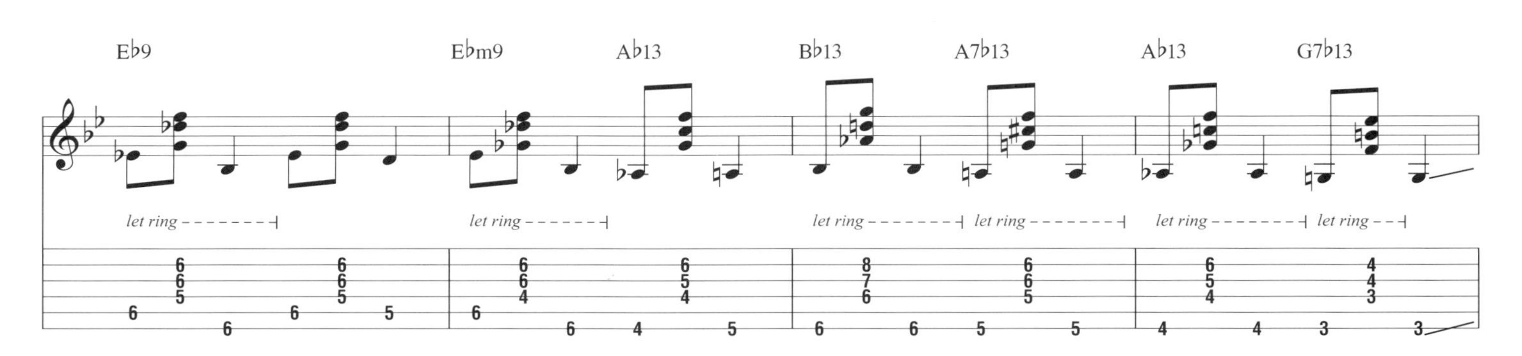

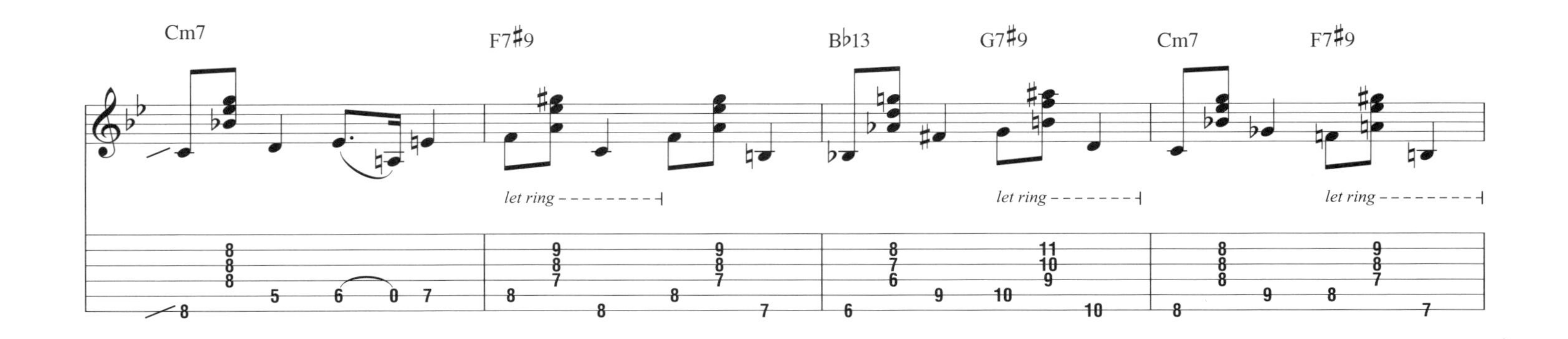
Cm7
F7♯9
B♭13
G7♯9
Cm7
F7♯9
let ring
let ring
let ring

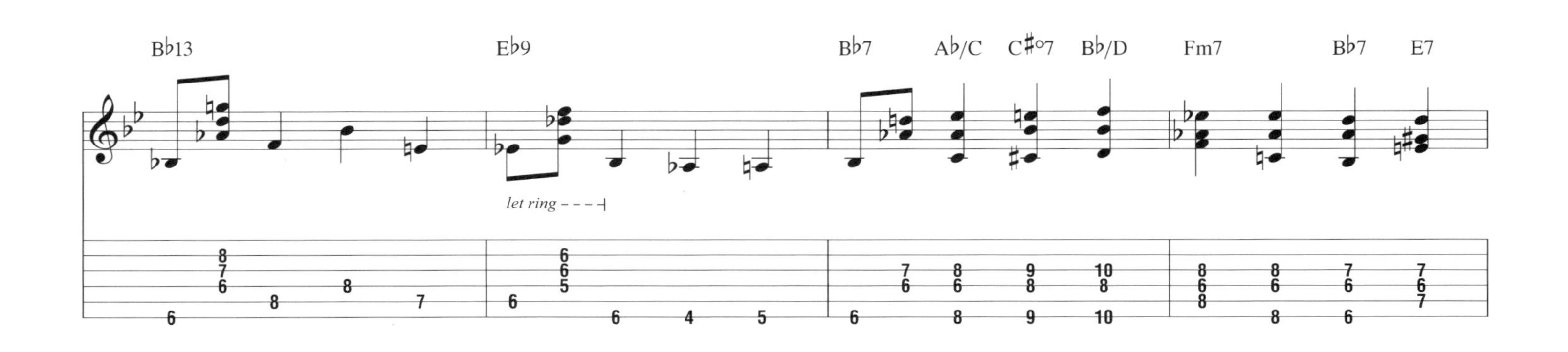
B♭13
E♭9
B♭7
A♭/C
C♯°7
B♭/D
Fm7
B♭7
E7
let ring

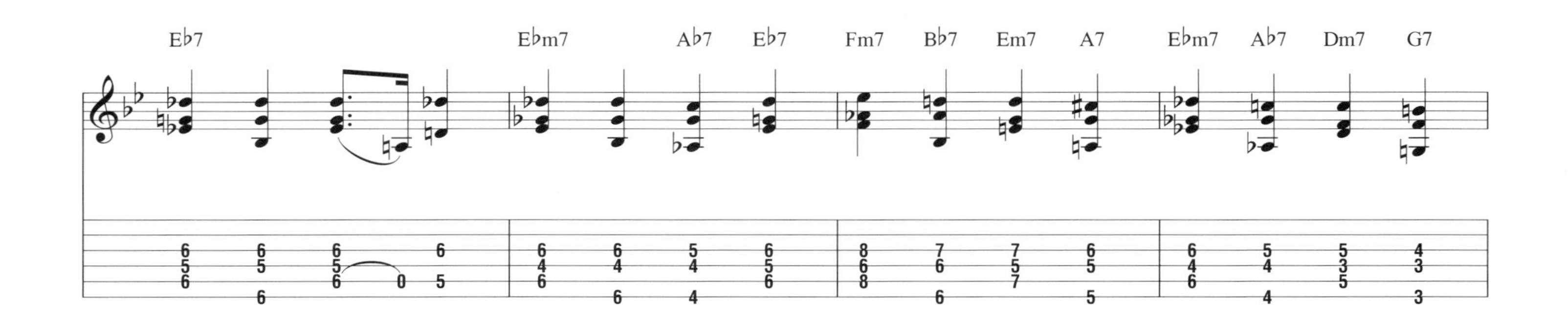
E♭7
E♭m7
A♭7
E♭7
Fm7
B♭7
Em7
A7
E♭m7
A♭7
Dm7
G7

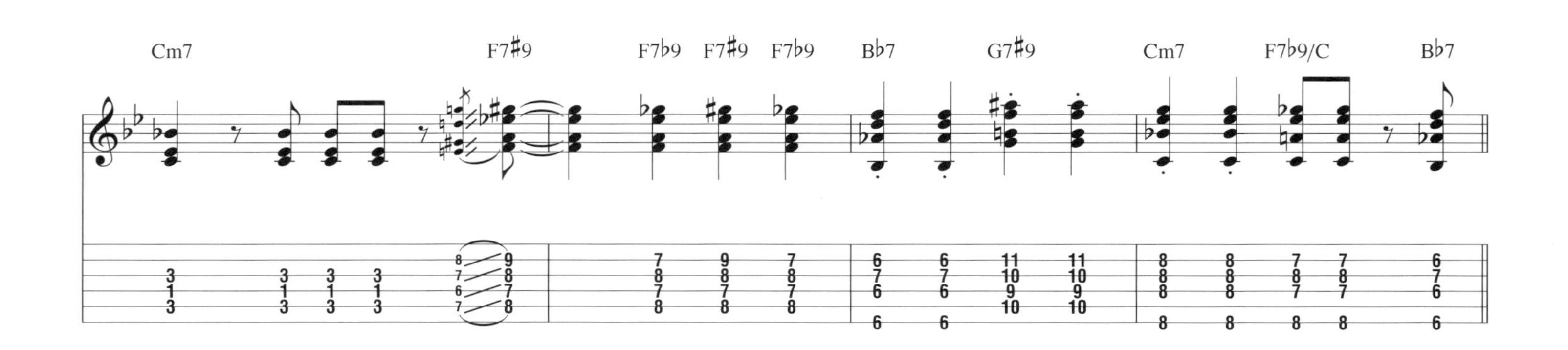
Cm7
F7♯9
F7♭9
F7♯9
F7♭9
B♭7
G7♯9
Cm7
F7♭9/C
B♭7

Example 18
(6:04)
B♭13 E♭9 B♭13 Fm9 B♭7♭13 E♭9
E♭m9 A♭13 B♭13 A7♭13 A♭13 G7♭13 Cm7 F7♯9
B♭13 G7♯9 Cm7 F7♭9 B♭13 E♭9 B♭13
Fm9 B♭7♭13 E♭9 E♭m9 A♭13 B♭13 A7♭13 A♭13 G7♭13
Cm7 F7♯9 B♭13 G7♯9 Cm7 F7♭9

Example 19
(12:08)

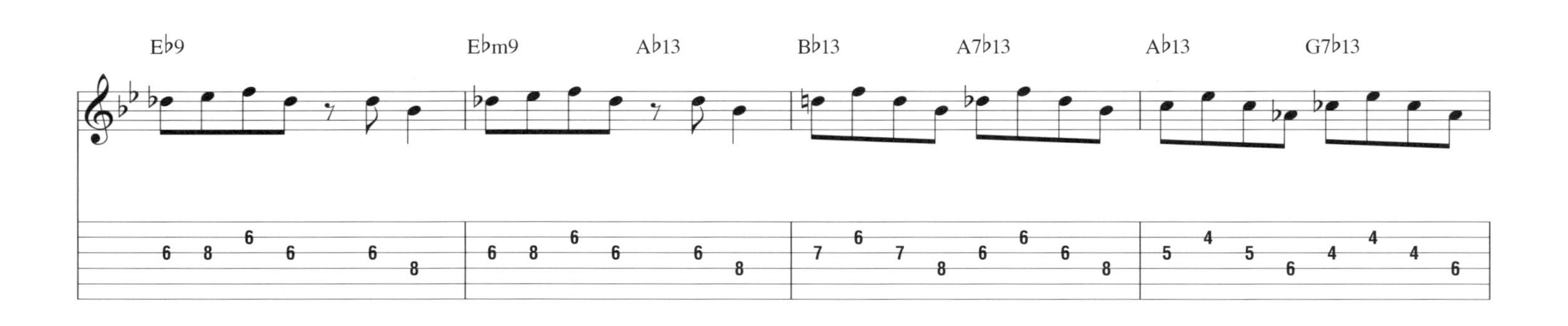

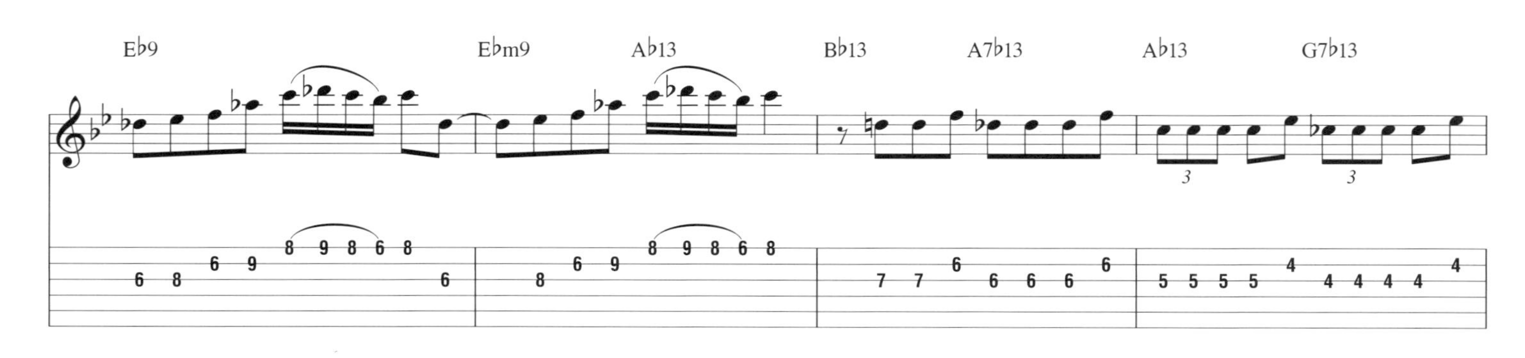

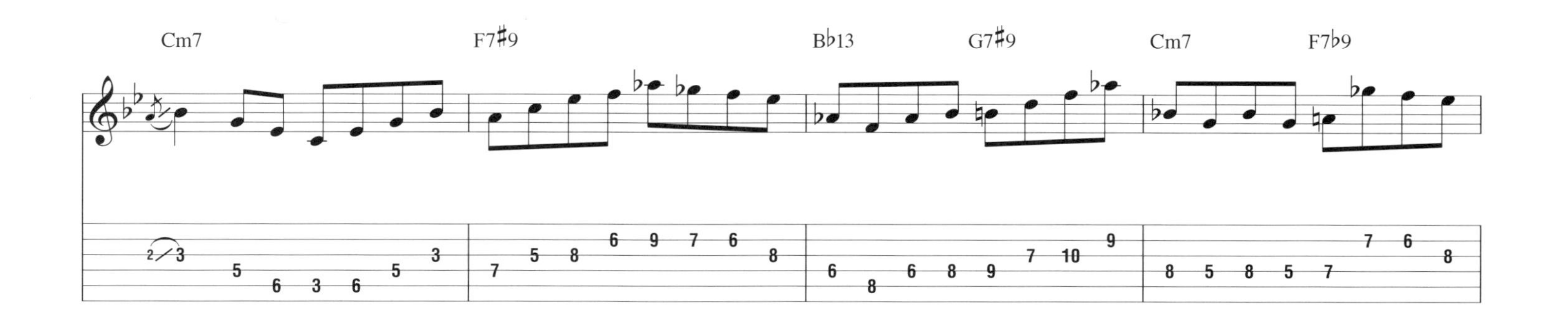
Cm7
F7♯9
B♭13
G7♯9
Cm7
F7♭9

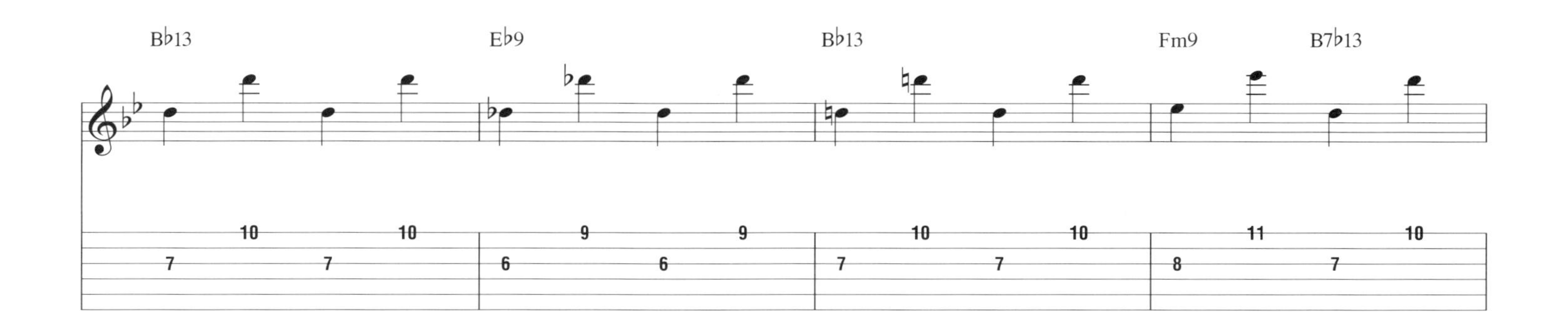
B♭13
E♭9
B♭13
Fm9
B7♭13

E♭9
E♭m7
A♭13
B♭13
A7♭13
A♭13
G7♭13

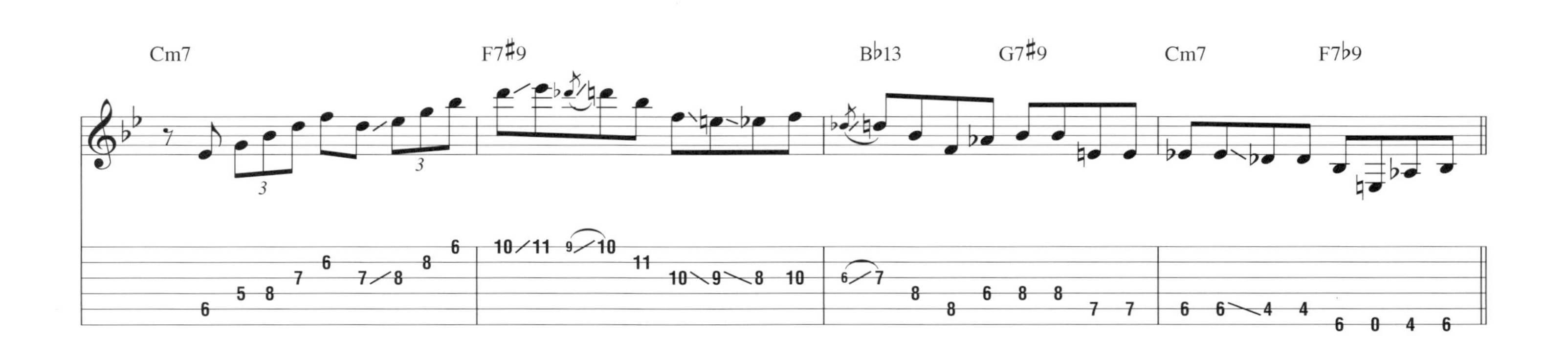
Cm7
F7♯9
B♭13
G7♯9
Cm7
F7♭9

Chapter 4: Developing Swing

Example 20
(2:03)

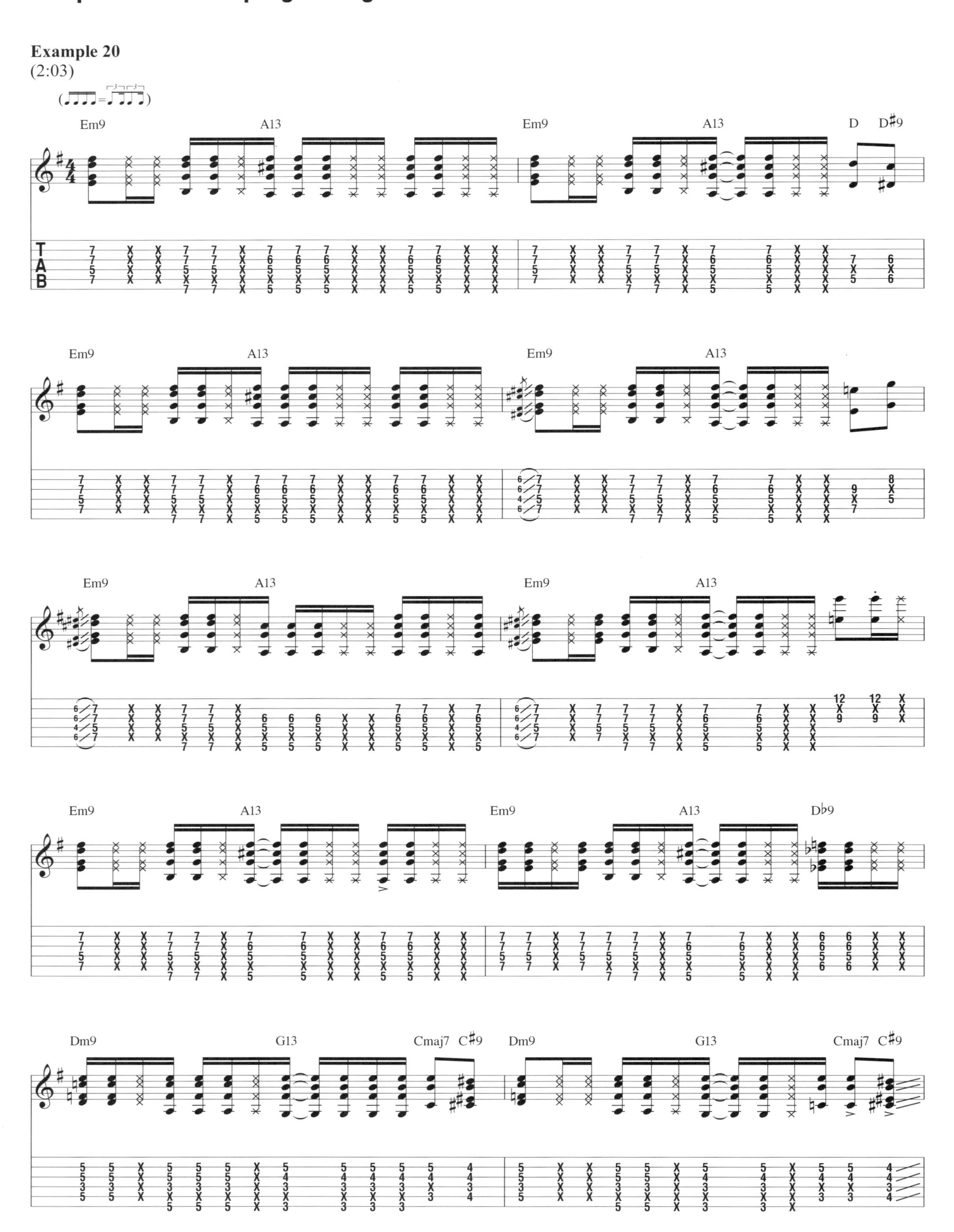

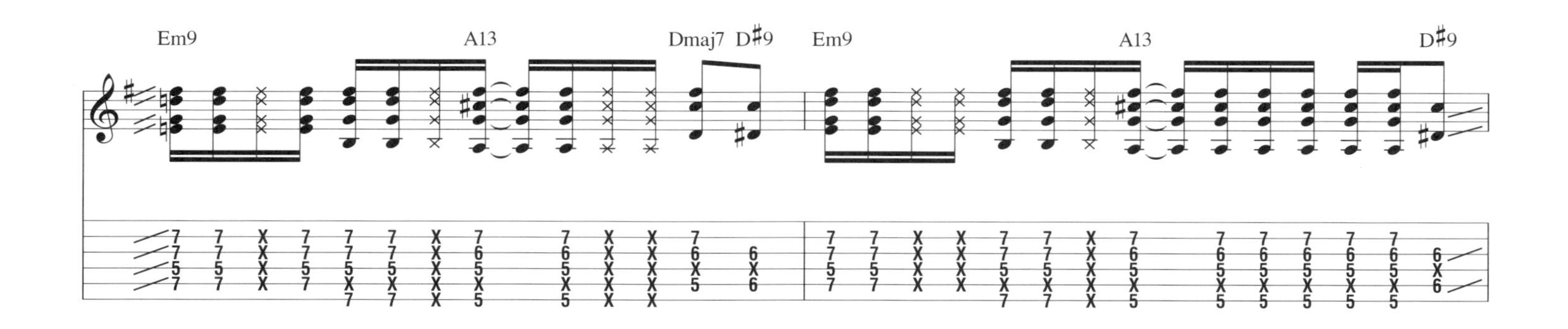
Em9
A13
Dmaj7
D♯9
Em9
A13
D♯9

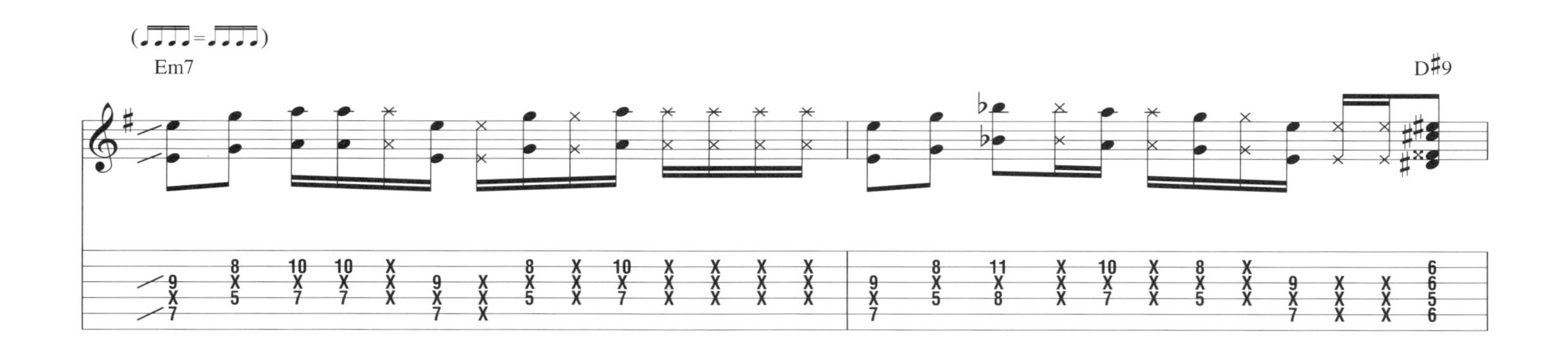
Em7
D♯9

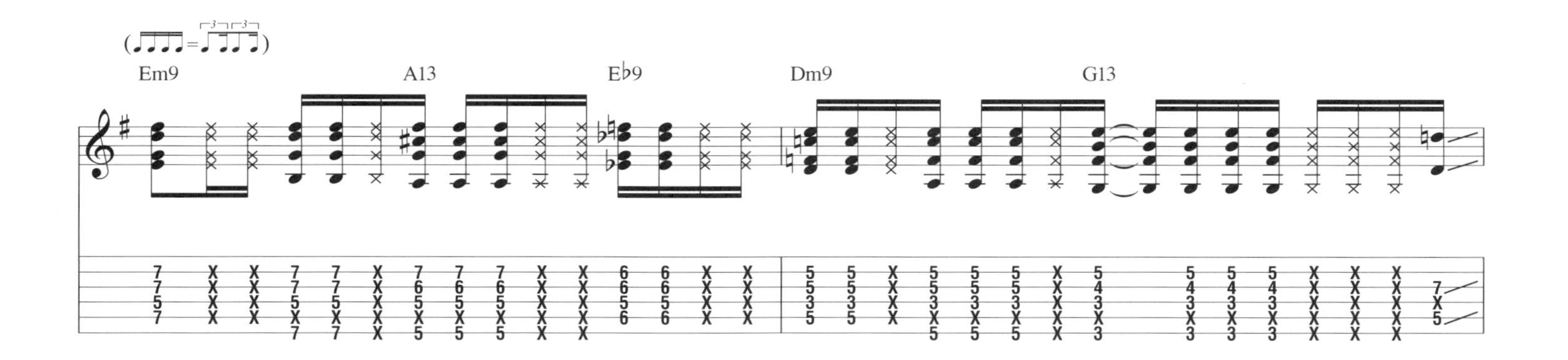
Em9
A13
E♭9
Dm9
G13

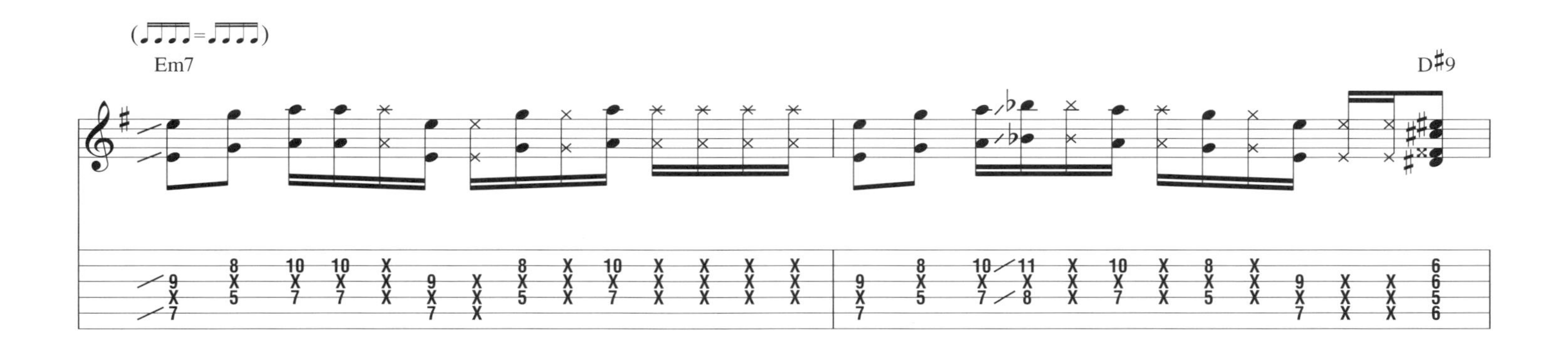
Em7
D♯9

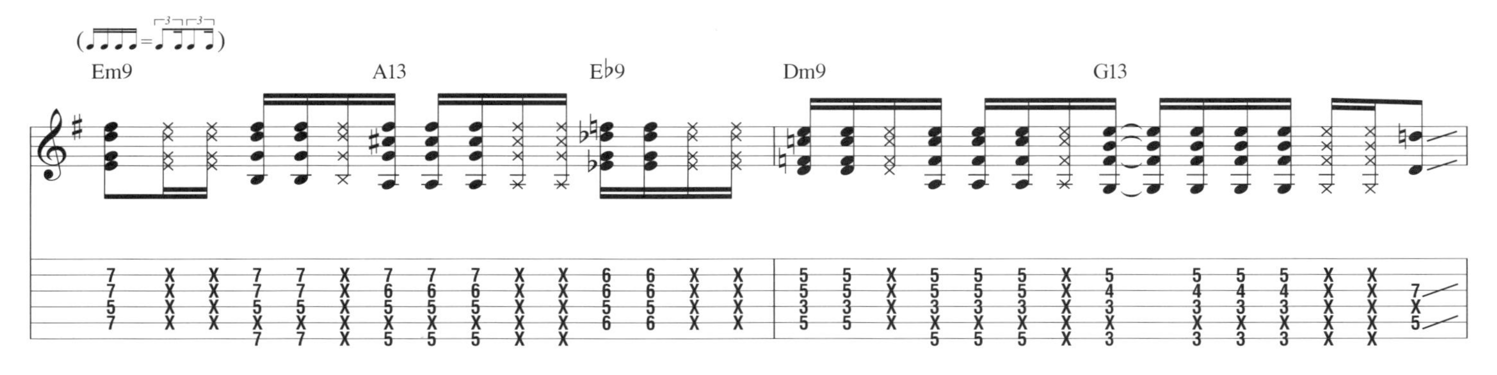
Em9
A13
E♭9
Dm9
G13

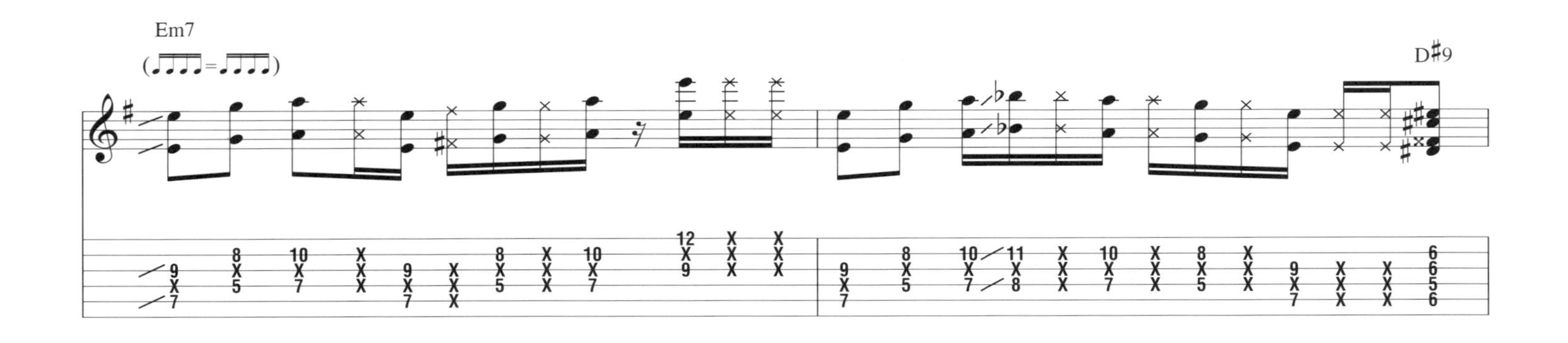
Em7
D♯9

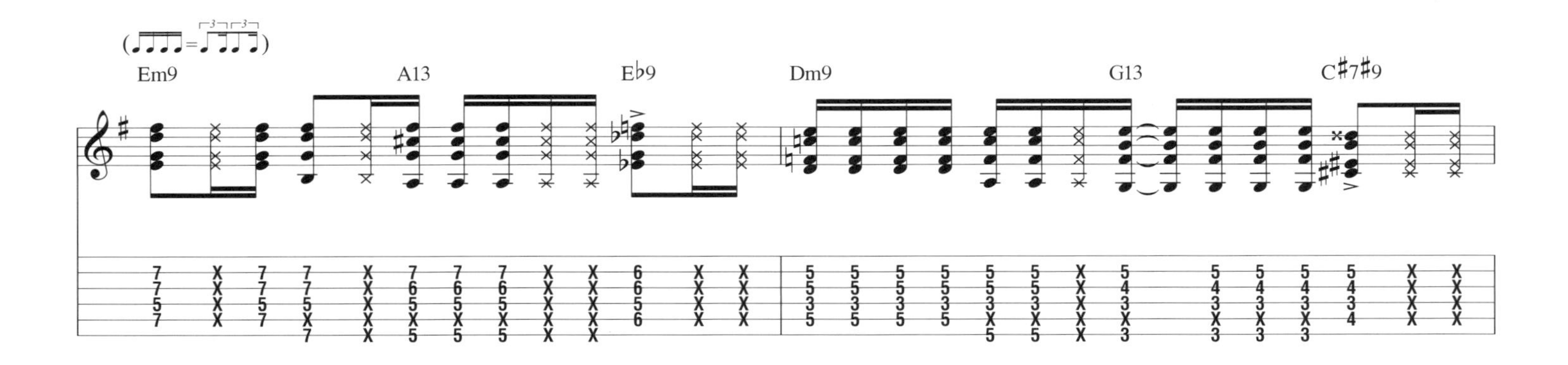
Em9
A13
E♭9
Dm9
G13
C♯7♯9

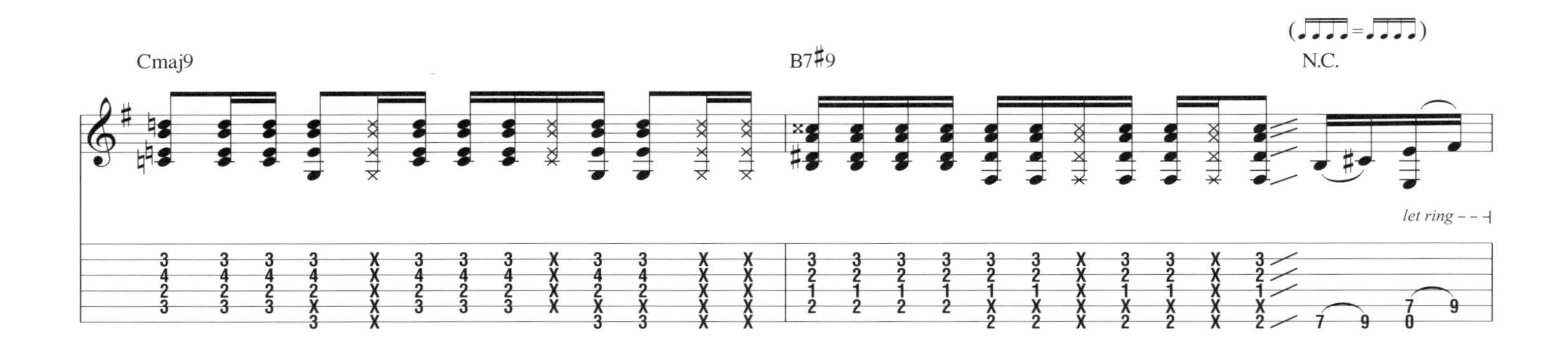
Cmaj9
B7♯9
N.C.
let ring

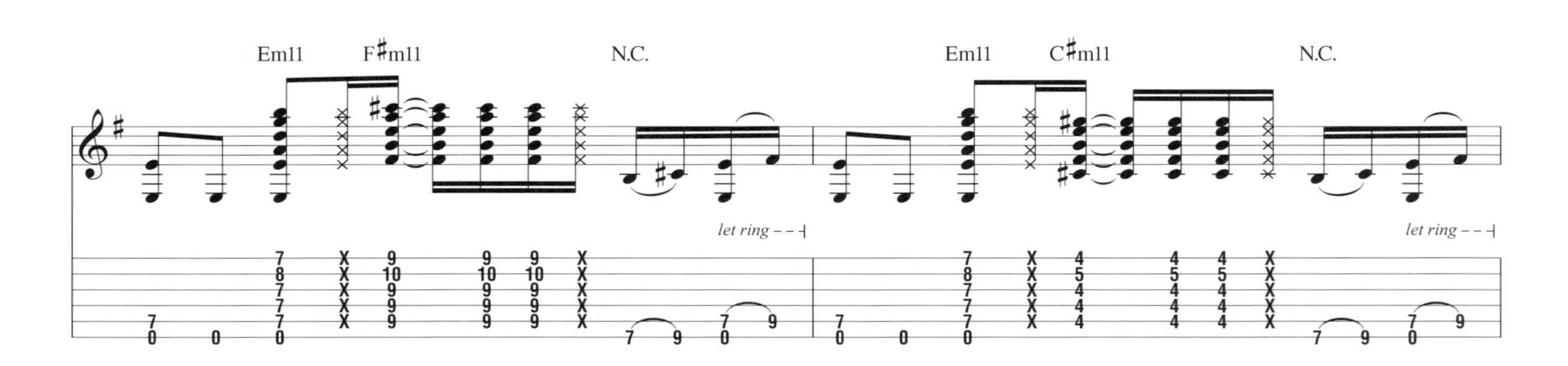
Em11
F♯m11
N.C.
let ring
Em11
C♯m11
N.C.
let ring

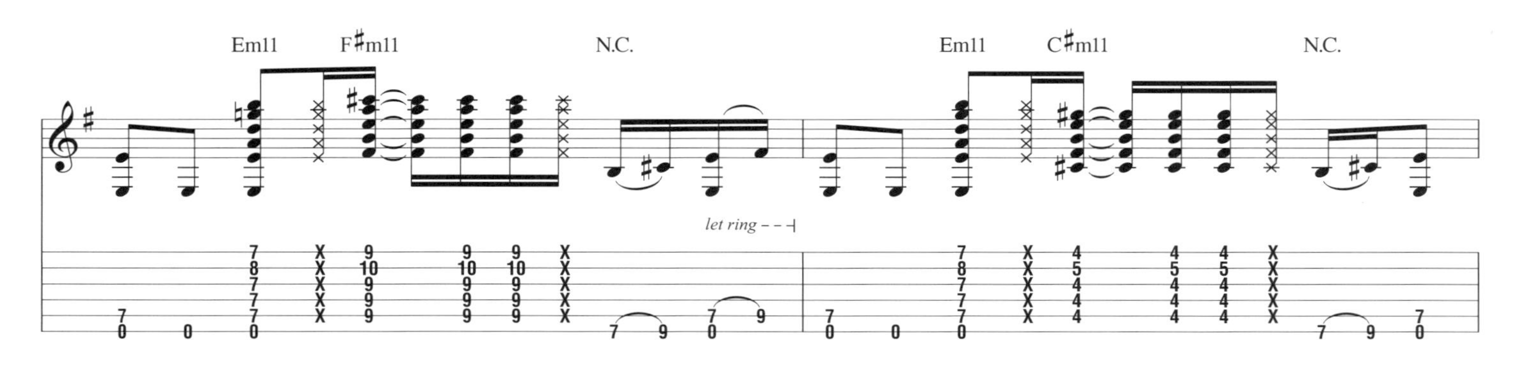
Em11
F♯m11
N.C.
let ring
Em11
C♯m11
N.C.

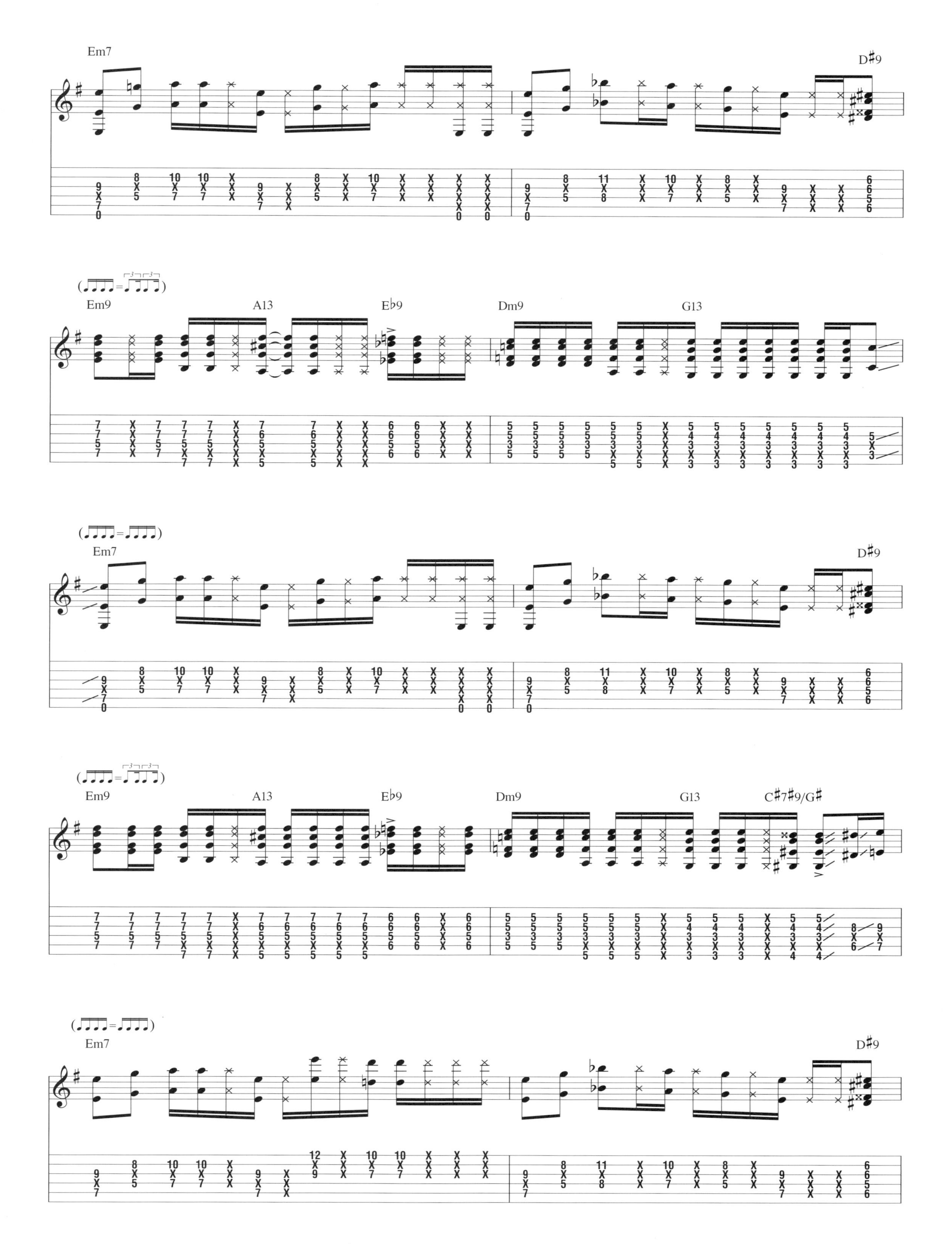
Em7
D♯9
Em9
A13
E♭9
Dm9
G13
Em7
D♯9
Em9
A13
E♭9
Dm9
G13
C♯7♯9/G♯
Em7
D♯9

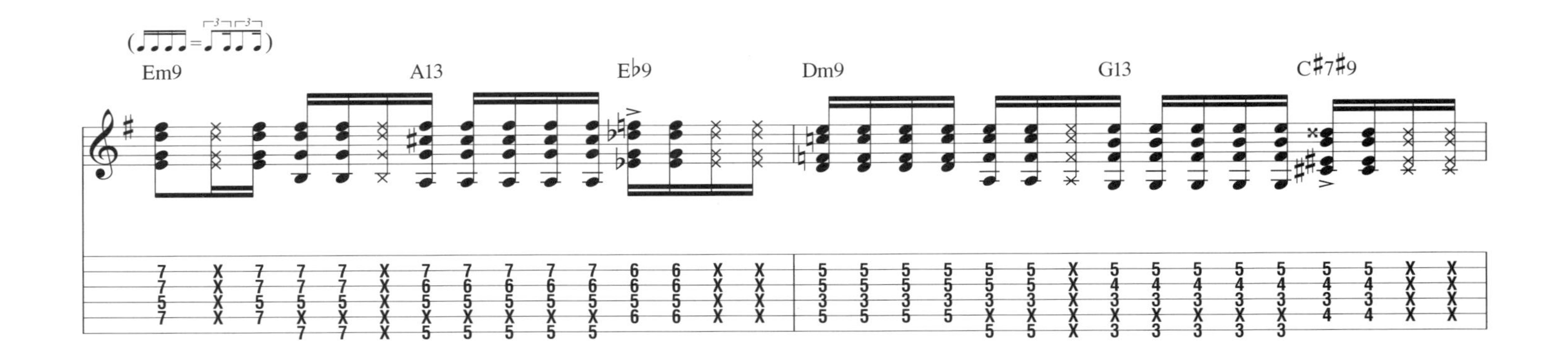
Em9
A13
E♭9
Dm9
G13
C♯7♯9

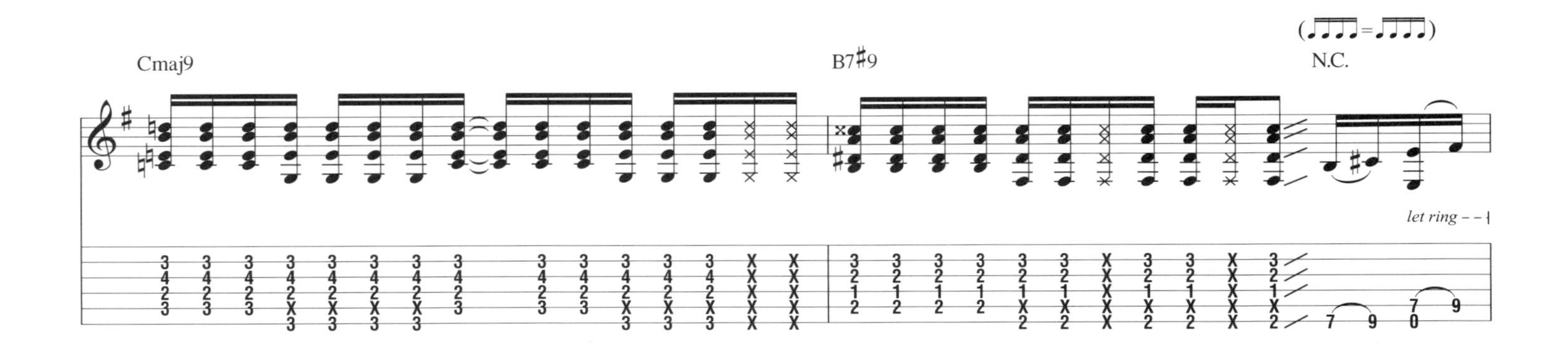
Cmaj9
B7♯9
N.C.
let ring

Em11
F♯m11
N.C.
let ring
Em11
C♯m11
grad. decres.
N.C.
let ring

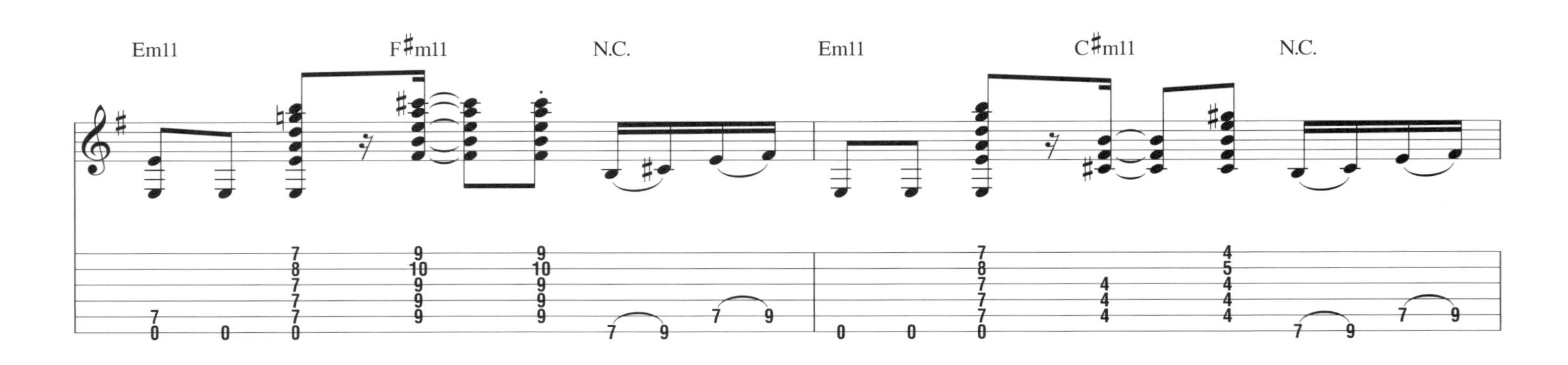
Em11
F♯m11
N.C.
Em11
C♯m11
N.C.

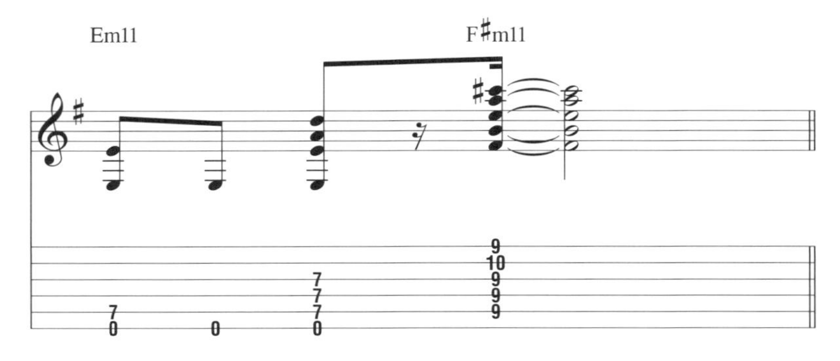
Em11
F♯m11

Chapter 5: Octaves

Example 21
(0:22)

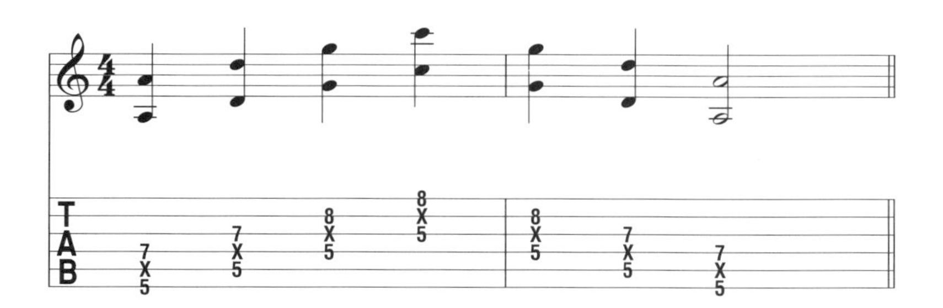

Example 22
(0:41)

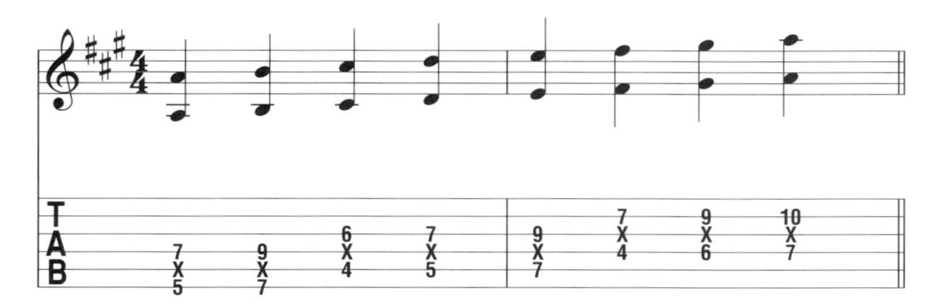

Example 23
(2:37)

N.C.

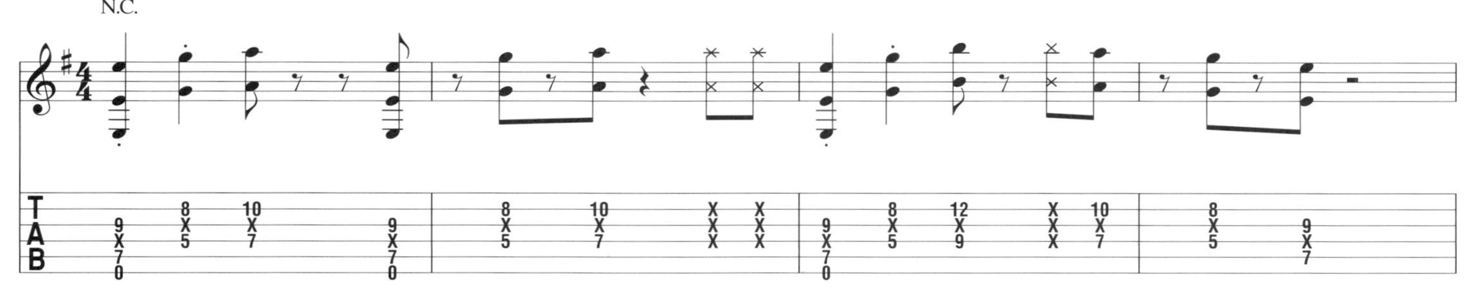

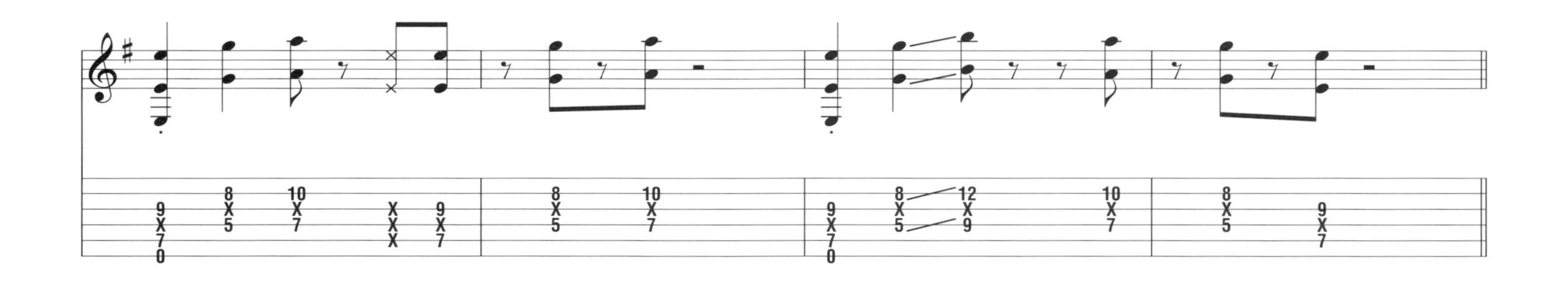

Example 24
(4:03)

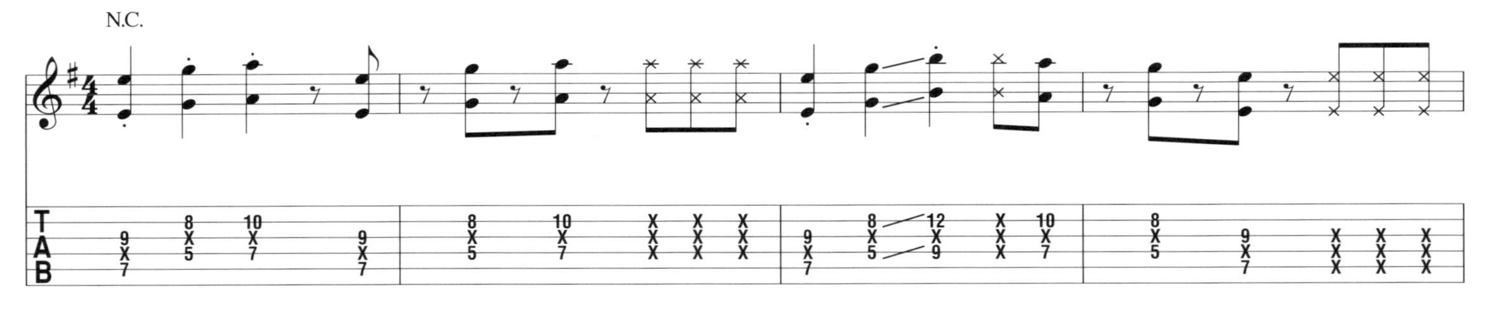

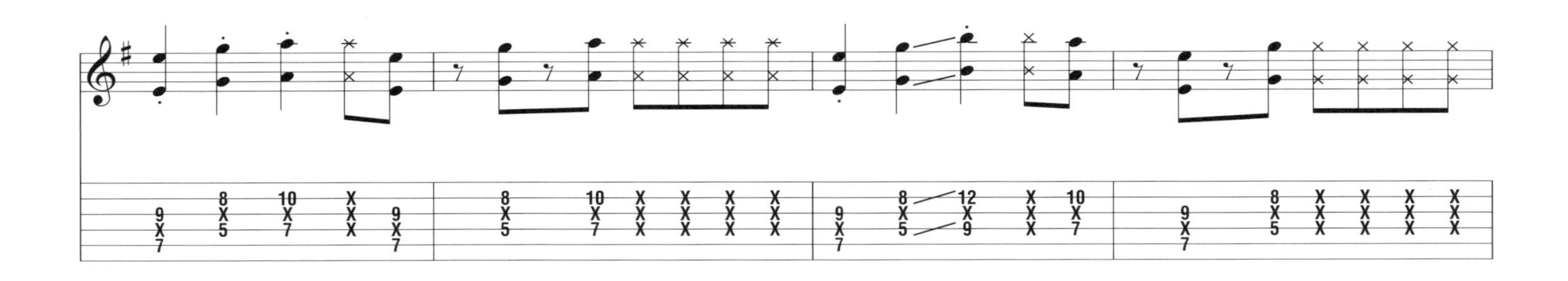

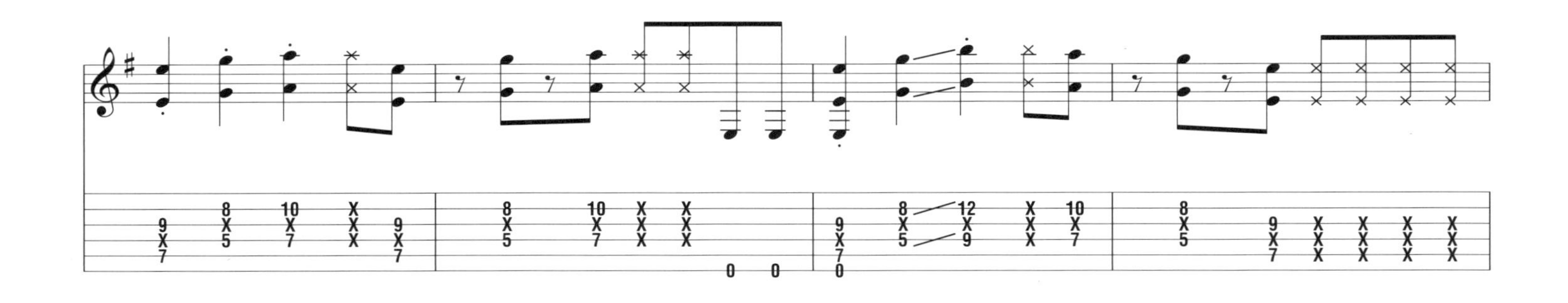

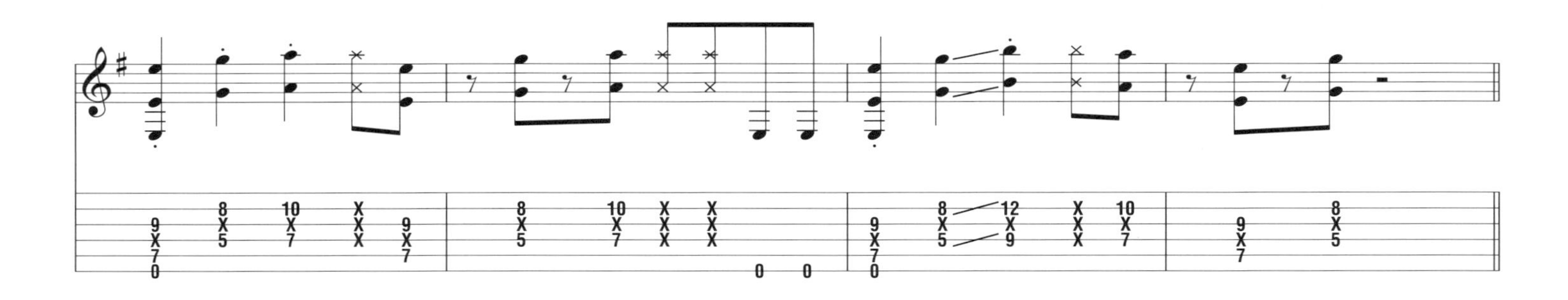

Example 25
(4:52)

N.C.

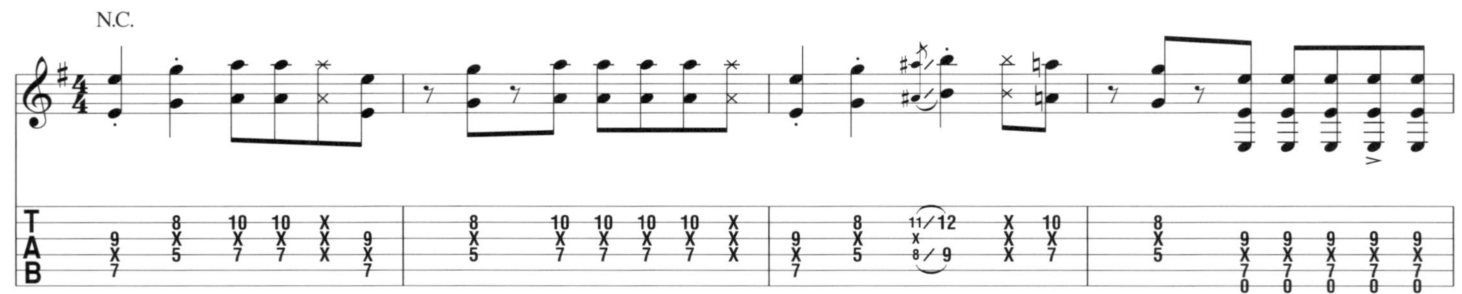

Chapter 6: Transcribing Licks

Example 26
(1:13)

Example 27
(1:27)

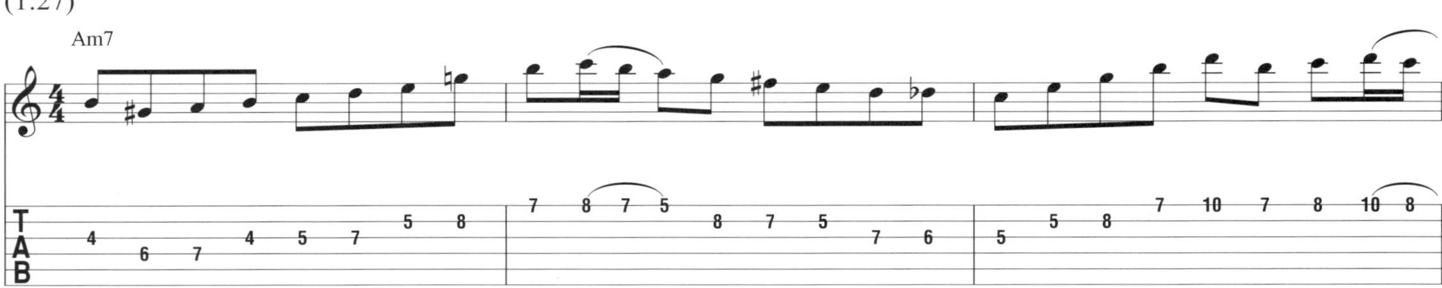

Example 28
(1:41)

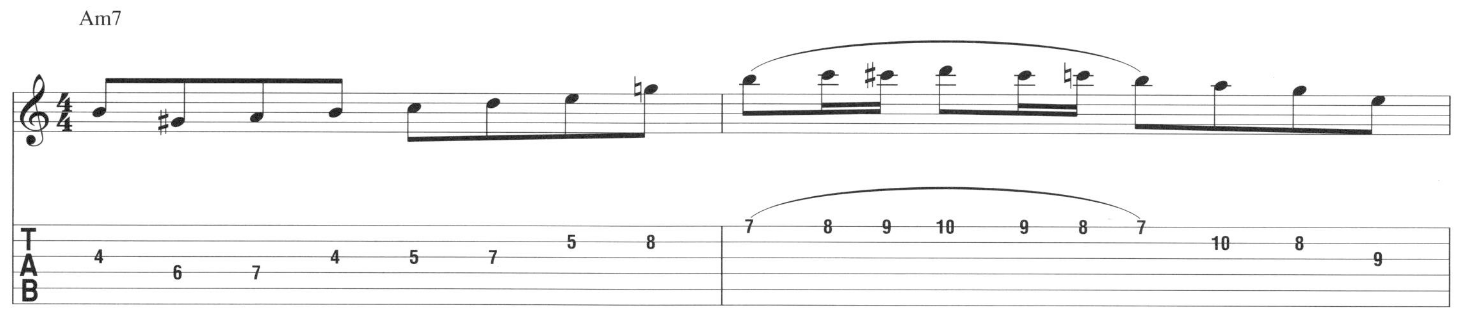

Outro

Example 29
(0:00)

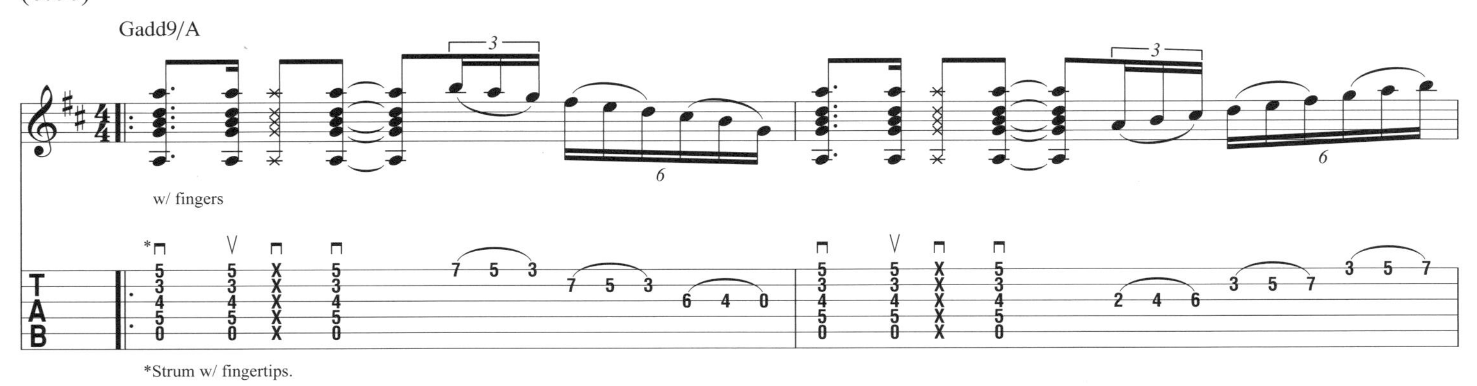

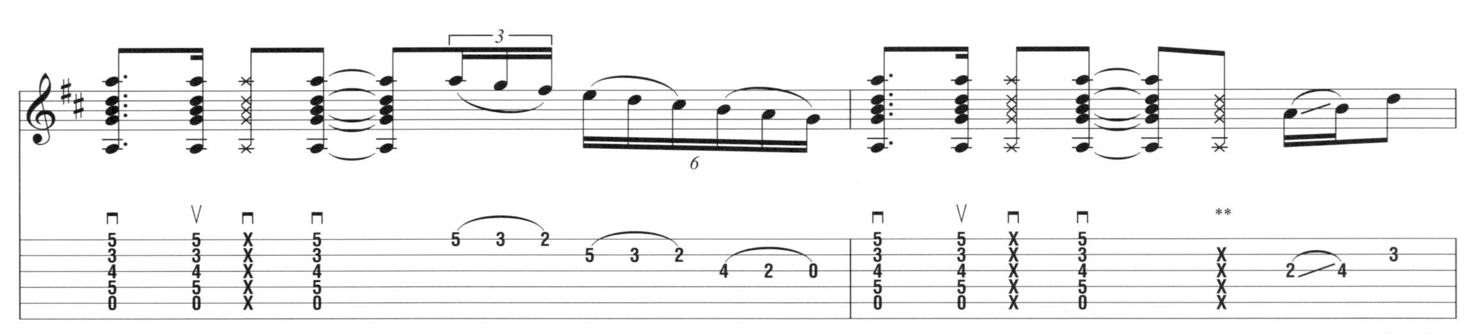

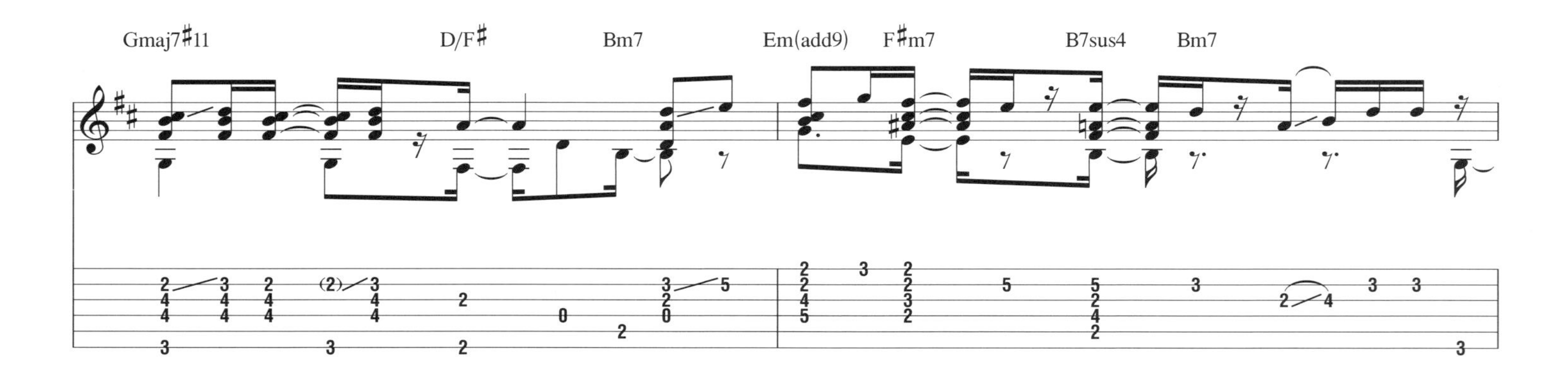

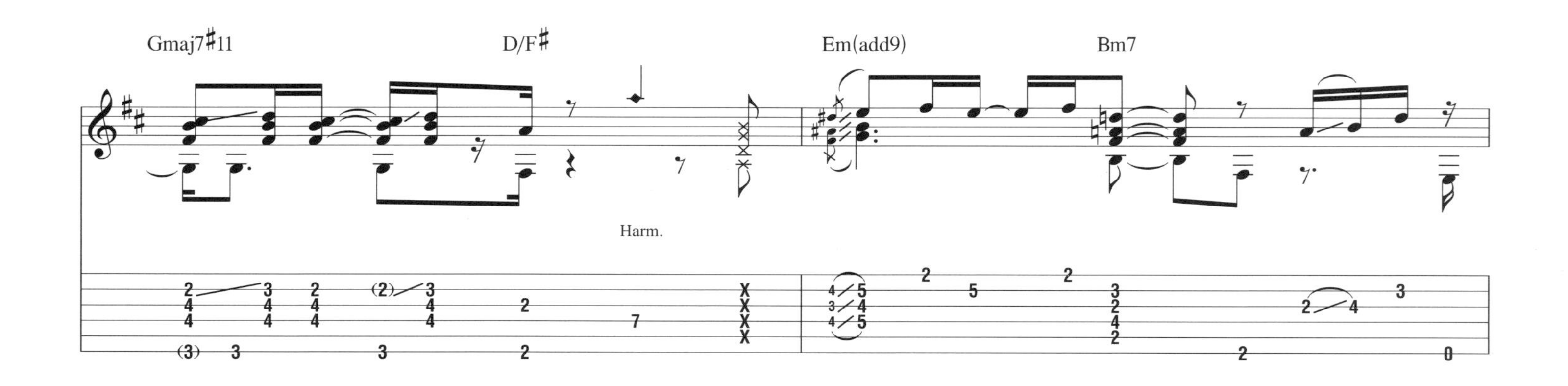

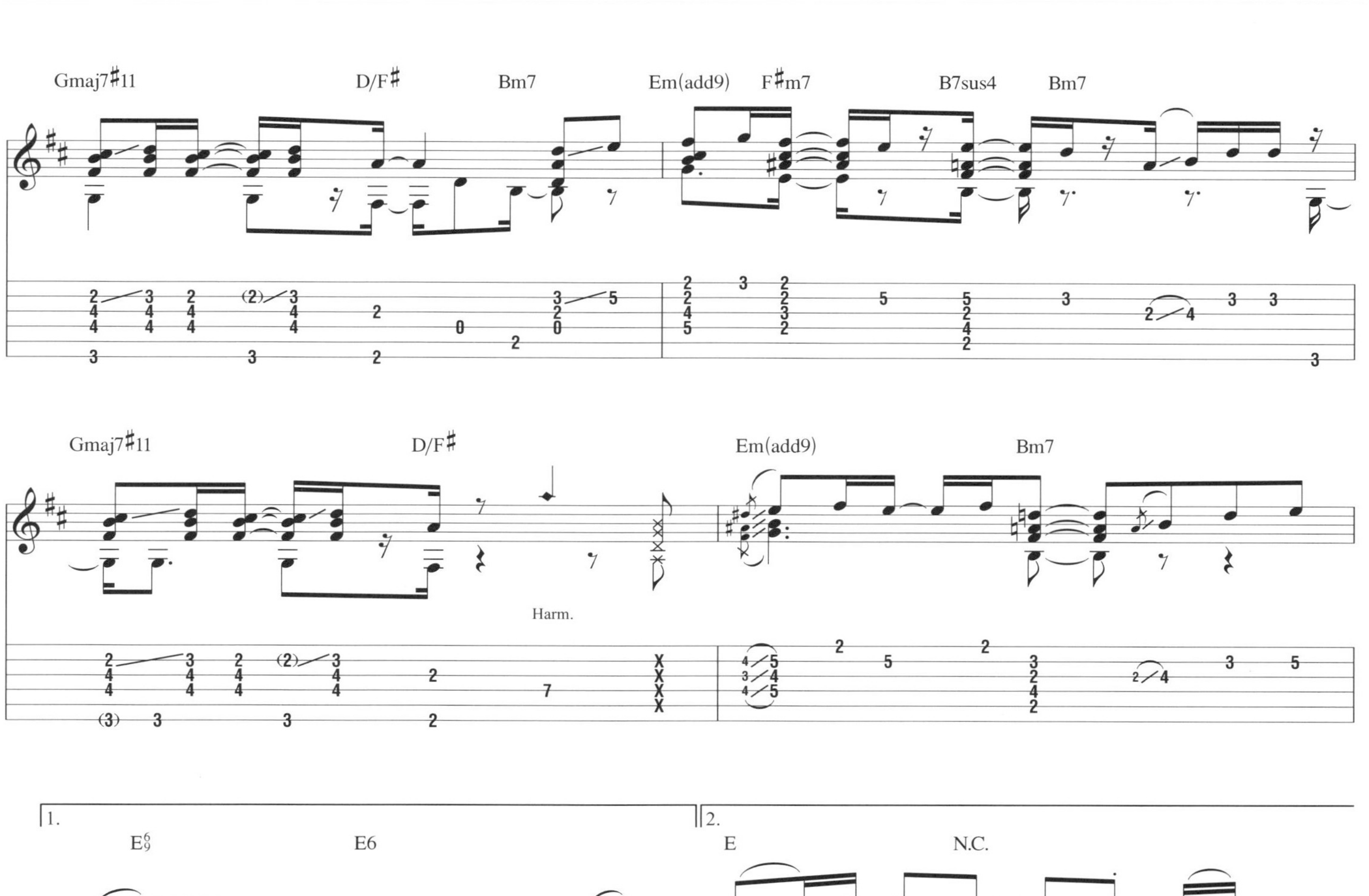
Gmaj7♯11
D/F♯
Bm7
Em(add9)
F♯m7
B7sus4
Bm7
Gmaj7♯11
D/F♯
Harm.
Em(add9)
Bm7

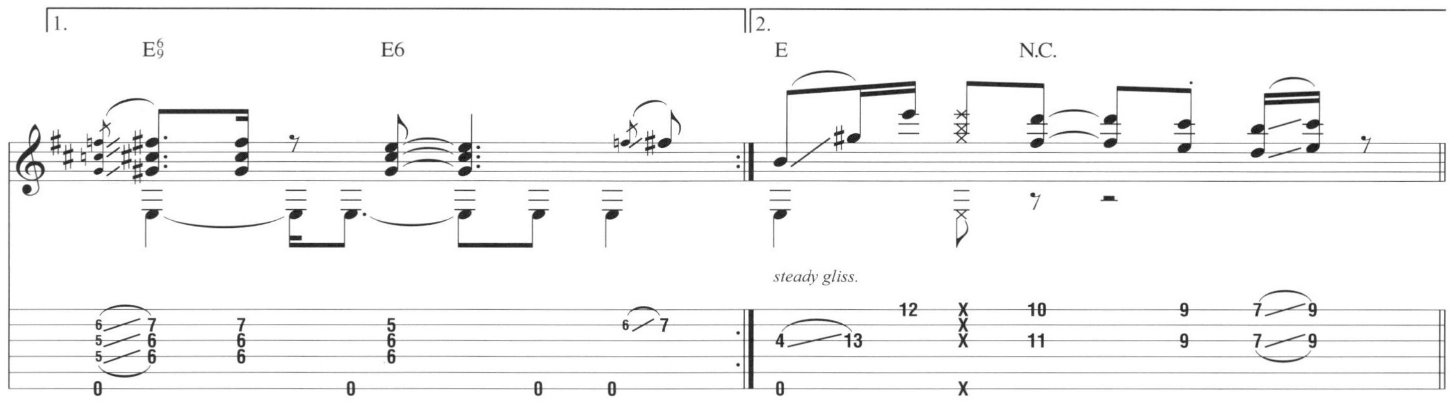
1.
E6/9
E6
2.
E
N.C.
steady gliss.

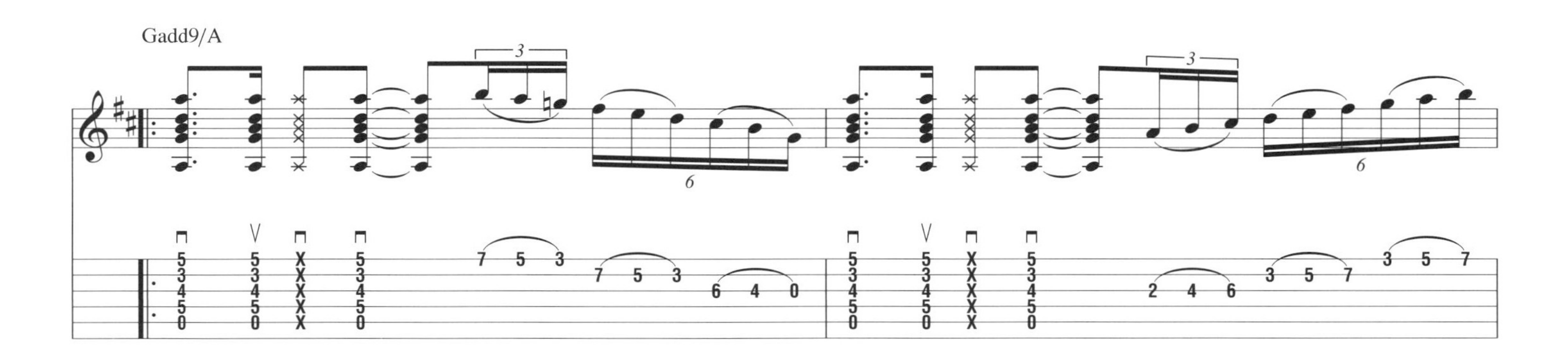
Gadd9/A

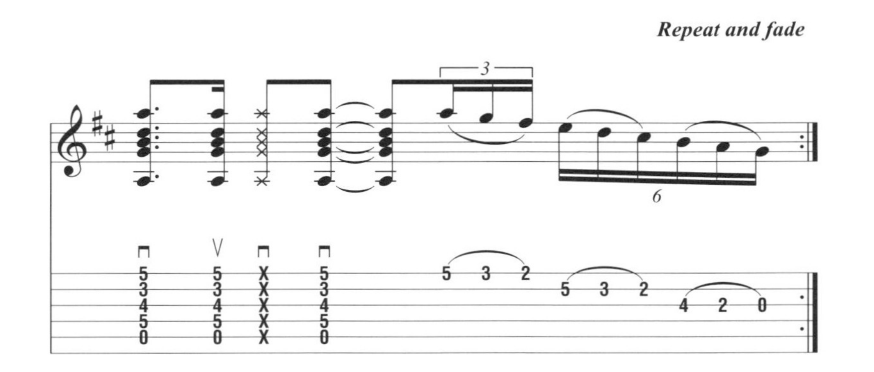
Repeat and fade

GUITAR NOTATION LEGEND

Guitar music can be notated three different ways: on a *musical staff*, in *tablature*, and in *rhythm slashes*.

RHYTHM SLASHES are written above the staff. Strum chords in the rhythm indicated. Use the chord diagrams found at the top of the first page of the transcription for the appropriate chord voicings. Round noteheads indicate single notes.

THE MUSICAL STAFF shows pitches and rhythms and is divided by bar lines into measures. Pitches are named after the first seven letters of the alphabet.

TABLATURE graphically represents the guitar fingerboard. Each horizontal line represents a string, and each number represents a fret.

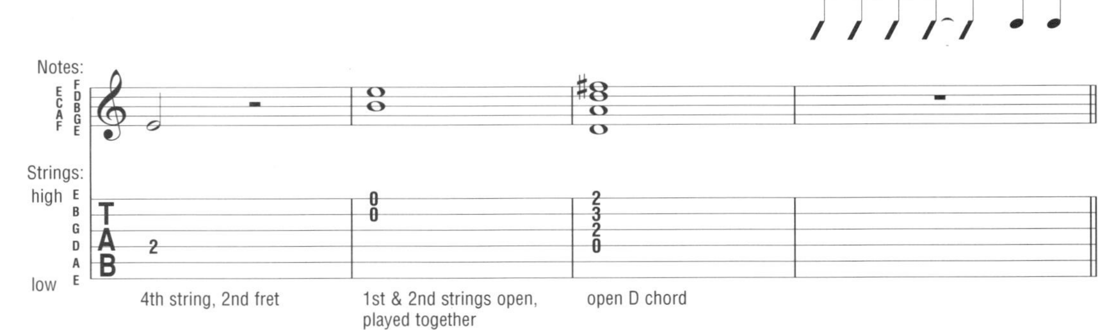

HALF-STEP BEND: Strike the note and bend up 1/2 step.

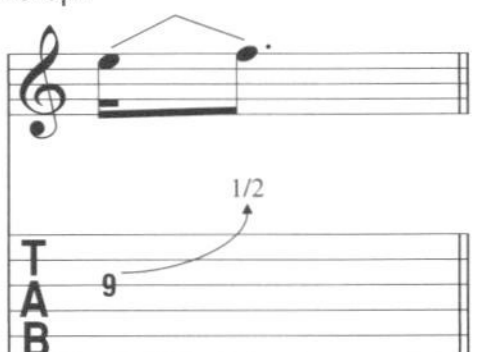

WHOLE-STEP BEND: Strike the note and bend up one step.

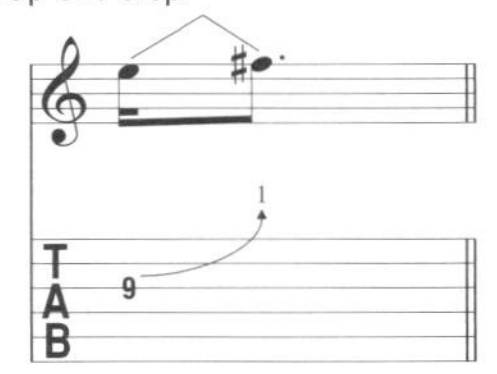

GRACE NOTE BEND: Strike the note and immediately bend up as indicated.

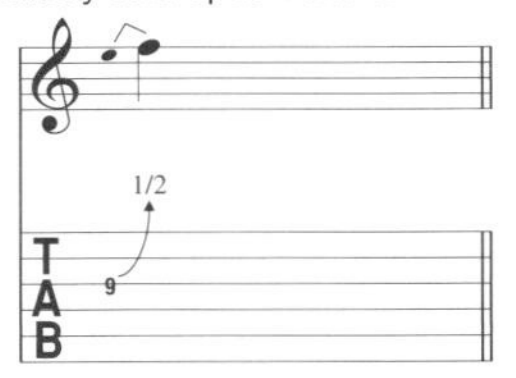

SLIGHT (MICROTONE) BEND: Strike the note and bend up 1/4 step.

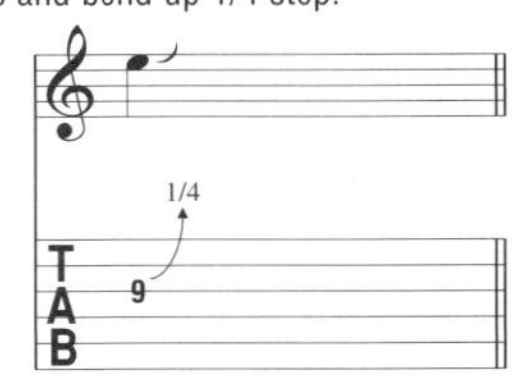

BEND AND RELEASE: Strike the note and bend up as indicated, then release back to the original note. Only the first note is struck.

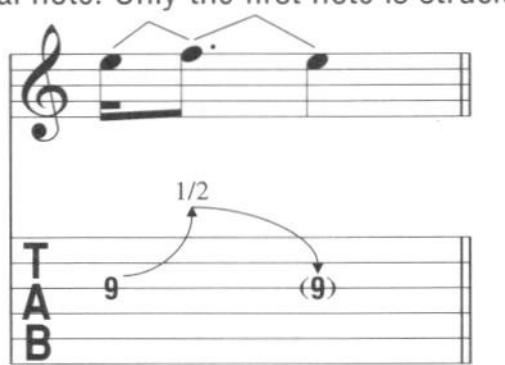

PRE-BEND: Bend the note as indicated, then strike it.

VIBRATO: The string is vibrated by rapidly bending and releasing the note with the fretting hand.

WIDE VIBRATO: The pitch is varied to a greater degree by vibrating with the fretting hand.

HAMMER-ON: Strike the first (lower) note with one finger, then sound the higher note (on the same string) with another finger by fretting it without picking.

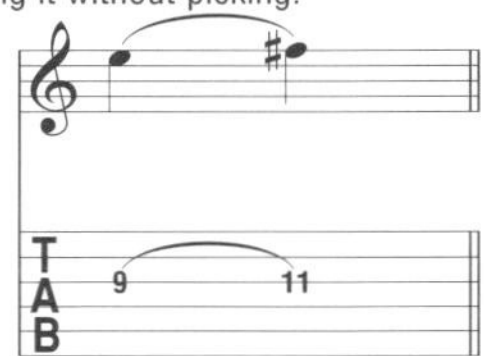

PULL-OFF: Place both fingers on the notes to be sounded. Strike the first note and without picking, pull the finger off to sound the second (lower) note.

LEGATO SLIDE: Strike the first note and then slide the same fret-hand finger up or down to the second note. The second note is not struck.

SHIFT SLIDE: Same as legato slide, except the second note is struck.

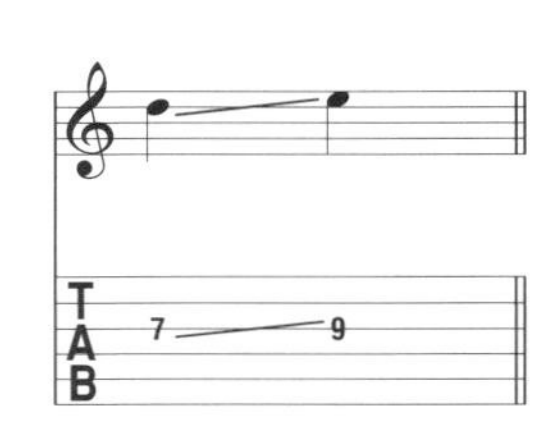

TRILL: Very rapidly alternate between the notes indicated by continuously hammering on and pulling off.

TAPPING: Hammer ("tap") the fret indicated with the pick-hand index or middle finger and pull off to the note fretted by the fret hand.

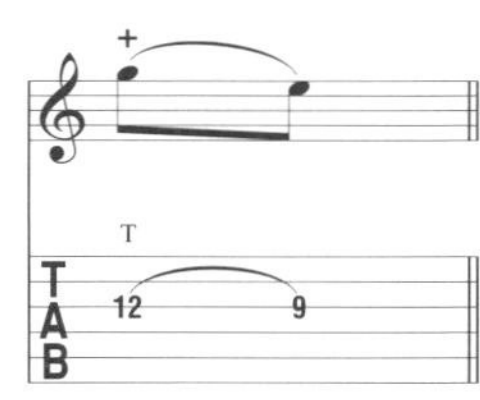

NATURAL HARMONIC: Strike the note while the fret-hand lightly touches the string directly over the fret indicated.

PINCH HARMONIC: The note is fretted normally and a harmonic is produced by adding the edge of the thumb or the tip of the index finger of the pick hand to the normal pick attack.

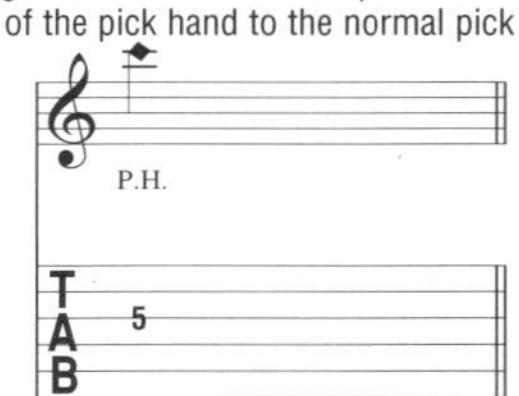

PICK SCRAPE: The edge of the pick is rubbed down (or up) the string, producing a scratchy sound.

MUFFLED STRINGS: A percussive sound is produced by laying the fret hand across the string(s) without depressing, and striking them with the pick hand.

PALM MUTING: The note is partially muted by the pick hand lightly touching the string(s) just before the bridge.

RAKE: Drag the pick across the strings indicated with a single motion.

TREMOLO PICKING: The note is picked as rapidly and continuously as possible.

VIBRATO BAR DIVE AND RETURN: The pitch of the note or chord is dropped a specified number of steps (in rhythm), then returned to the original pitch.

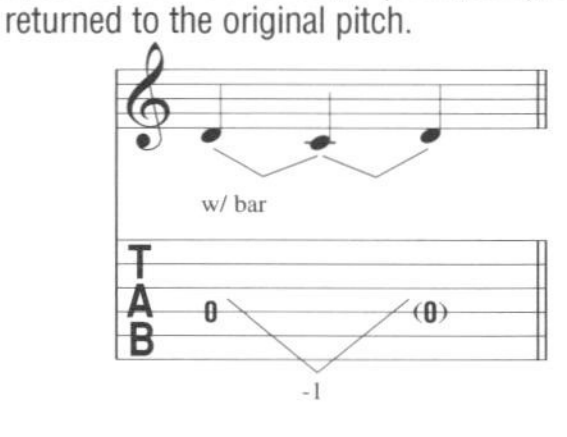

VIBRATO BAR SCOOP: Depress the bar just before striking the note, then quickly release the bar.

VIBRATO BAR DIP: Strike the note and then immediately drop a specified number of steps, then release back to the original pitch.

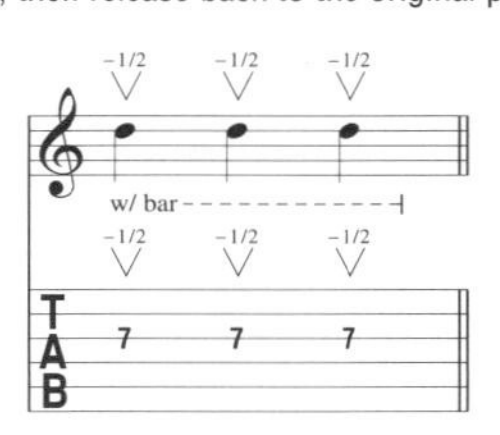